kylie
showgirl
The Unofficial Biography!

Kylie

Photo: Kenneth Prater Photography

Bryony Sutherland and **Lucy Ellis**
both live and work in London.
Previous books for Omnibus Press are
Annie Lennox – The Biography,
Tom Jones – Close Up and *The Complete*
Guide To The Music Of George Michael
& Wham! Their forthcoming biography
on Nicole Kidman will be published by
Aurum Press in autumn 2002.
For more information visit
www.atomic2.pwp.blueyonder.co.uk

Atomic would like to thank Chris, Nikki,
Chloë, Melissa, Frankie, Elton, Anton,
John, Dad, Andrew and the Diva.
It's been great.

Bryony Sutherland & Lucy Ellis
January 2002

Copyright © 2002 Omnibus Press
(A Division of Music Sales Limited)

Cover & Book designed by Chloë Alexander
Picture research by Nikki Lloyd and Steve Behan

ISBN: 0.7119.9294.0
Order No: OP 48917

Printed and bound in U.K.
A catalogue record for this book is available from the British Library.

Visit Omnibus Press on the web at **www.omnibuspress.com**

Exclusive Distributors
Music Sales Limited,
8/9 Frith Street,
London W1D 3JB, UK.

Music Sales Corporation,
257 Park Avenue South,
New York, NY 10010, USA.

Macmillan Distribution Services,
53 Park West Drive,
Derrimut, Vic 3030,
Australia.

To the Music Trade only:
Music Sales Limited,
8/9 Frith Street,
London W1D 3JB, UK.

All pictures courtesty of
Alpha, All Action, Big Pictures, Camera Press, Corbis, Famous, Angela
Lubrano, London Features International, Photofeatures, Pictorial Press,
Press Association, Rex Features, S.I.N.

Every effort has been made to trace the copyright holders of the
photographs in this book but one or two were unreachable.
We would be grateful if the photographers concerned would contact us.

kylie
showgirl

The Unofficial Biography!

Bryony Sutherland
Lucy Ellis

Contents

Prologue: Come Into My World

Intro

"*I started out as the girl-next-door and people can still see that.*"

FROM RAMSEY STREET TO REIGNING POP queen, Kylie Ann Minogue proves that talent comes in tiny packages: "I started in TV when I was nine ... I was only a little smaller than I am now!"

Now known simply by her first name, the pint-sized Australian has sold well over 30 million records. Her recent number one single, 'Can't Get You Out Of My Head', was her 35th Top 20 hit. At the tender age of 34, the multi-millionairess is an icon worshipped by men and women alike, and feels "kind of humbled" by the generation of British teenagers called Kylie. She's so famous, she's virtually a trademark.

"I guess I'm attainable," says the former *Neighbours* star when quizzed on her enduring popularity. "I think it goes way back. The way the public perceive me isn't about today, it's about 16 years' worth of me. I started out as the girl-next-door and people can still see that.

"They've grown up with me and have seen me make a fool of myself; have many less-than-attractive moments style-wise, and generally gone through ups and downs in my career and relationships. People have seen that I'm fallible; that I'm not untouchable like the perfect supermodels in magazines.

"*I think they understand that if I were to pop round to their place in my tracksuit for a glass of wine, we'd get on*"

Basking in the aftermath of a sold-out tour promoting *Fever*, her latest chart-topping album, how does the star once nicknamed 'The Singing Budgie' by her critics justify her success?

"A lot of my career has been a happy accident. Something my dad said to me sticks because it's the story of my life: I skip steps one to eight and just do nine and 10, but miraculously, I get away with it." If her recent comeback is anything to go by, Kylie will "get away with it" for many years to come.

Kylie stole the show at the BRIT Awards in February 2002 in a stunning Dolce & Gabbana corset dress

Chapter 1: Step Back In Time

"On one hand there's this girl called Kylie and on the other there's Kylie The Star. I can't see her without thinking about where I came from and who I actually am. Sometimes 'she' is miles away from who I am."

KYLIE ANN MINOGUE WAS BORN AT THE Star of Bethlehem Hospital in Melbourne, Australia on May 28, 1968. Already petite, she weighed in at just 6 lbs. Her father, Ron, was a fifth-generation Australian accountant and her mother, Carol, a Welsh former ballerina who had traded in dancing for marriage. Within the next three years Kylie was joined by a younger brother, Brendan, and a sister, Danielle, known as 'Dannii'.

Apart from Auntie Suzette, an actress, Kylie's family led an average suburban life without the lure of fame. "It sounds like we were brought up in *The Waltons* or *The Brady Bunch*. But it's all true! I was brought up with my feet on the ground and I'm grateful for that. I wouldn't be in such a good way if I hadn't had that upbringing. My parents aren't at all interested in showbiz."

When asked which characteristics she inherited from her parents, Kylie offers two extremes that form an unlikely balance.

"My mother is very compassionate and gentle, so I've probably got that from her.

My dad is very businesslike, and I can't stand incompetence in people."

Kylie's exhibitionist streak emerged from a young age. "I thought I was shy, but my mum said that when I was really tiny I was a poser," she says. "I would always be doing expressive things with my hands."

Showing an early interest in music, Kylie went to classes at the age of four, "banging on sticks and glockenspiels and stuff like that. And I learned the violin, the most teeny, teeny kiddie violin with little Band Aid strips to show where your fingers go. Then I moved on to piano, which I did from seven or eight till about 13." Kylie also studied flute but was a lazy

scholar, avoiding practice at all costs. "I was a good mimic," she admits. "I learned everything by ear."

Her talents did not go unnoticed. "My mother tells this story about me competing in the under-eights piano competition at the Dandenong Eisteddford. Apparently I walked on stage, turned and gave a big smile to the judges, then proceeded to play 'Run Rabbit Run'. As I walked off the stage, I gave the judge another big smile. My mum is sure I only came second because of the smile, not because of the piano-playing. Even then I must've been thinking: 'Work on the charm, kid! Work on the charm!'"

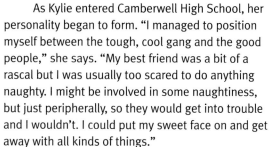

Above: Kylie and her brother, Brendan
Below: Olivia Newton-John models skin-tight pants in *Grease*

As Kylie entered Camberwell High School, her personality began to form. "I managed to position myself between the tough, cool gang and the good people," she says. "My best friend was a bit of a rascal but I was usually too scared to do anything naughty. I might be involved in some naughtiness, but just peripherally, so they would get into trouble and I wouldn't. I could put my sweet face on and get away with all kinds of things."

Academically it soon became clear Kylie's leanings were strongly towards the arts. "I liked those subjects I think everyone would like – graphics, art," she recalls. "I had no interest in science. It was Bunsen burners and sheep's eyeballs. I had to cut them up. It was awful. An eyeball, looking at you. It was really hard to cut, it went all over the place. I didn't want anything to do with it!

"I wasn't really clever but I wasn't stupid. But even at primary school, I was more of a homey, crafty person. I'd rather sit and do something like sewing.

❝I liked reading rather than going out and playing netball.❞

Initially Kylie fancied herself as a singer. "I do remember being little and singing into the hairbrush," she confesses. "I'd sing along to The Beatles and the Stones, to one Bonnie Tyler song I absolutely loved. But I never really had any aspiration to be on TV."

Nevertheless, a year or so later, Kylie was bitten by the acting bug. The trigger was the hugely successful musical, *Grease*.

❝I remember that Grease inspired me like nothing else❞

I just wished to be like Olivia Newton-John in her skin-tight pants in that tunnel with John Travolta."

In March 1979 Kylie's visions of stardom began to take shape. Dannii, herself a budding actress, had been told by their aunt about an upcoming role as a Dutch girl named Carla in the high profile Australian soap, *The Sullivans*. In persuading her mother to take her to the audition, Dannii's biggest mistake was allowing her 10-year-old sister to come along for the ride. As soon as the casting director saw Kylie, the decision was made. Carol Minogue was left to pick up the pieces, explaining to the distraught Dannii that her sister had more experience and she should be pleased for her.

Unfortunately Kylie's only recollection of her role in *The Sullivans* is that, "I had to speak in a Dutch accent, which I wasn't very good at." Poor Dannii later appeared on the same show, as a Carla lookalike.

After Kylie's 11th birthday she landed a one-off appearance in the airport melodrama, *Skyways*. This job was not so memorable for her portrayal of a tetchy girl called Robin, more for a portentous meeting with another child actor, who played her brother. His name: Jason Donovan.

Indeed, Kylie's diminutive stature (5'1") affected her at times. "I wasn't sporty because of my little legs, and couldn't run very fast. But I was well treated by the other kids because I was the smallest thing ever."

She met her first proper boyfriend, David Wood, in her early teens. "I'd fancied the pants off this guy for ages. He was a bit of a rebel and I thought he was quite exotic with his crazy, curly black hair." Kylie risked a telling-off at the local swimming pool to steal her first kiss. "The signs were always very clear: No Necking, Ducking or Bombing. There was definitely no bombing allowed because David did one and got sent on garbage duty, clearing up trash. Because I fancied him, I went around with him and got to pick up rubbish. And then we kissed.

"Prior to that I'd been consumed with all the usual concerns of a normal 13-year-old before their first kiss, like having to practise on your hand, wondering what happens and asking your friends, 'What goes on in there?' But it was a good kiss." David was to remain a fairly constant companion for the next four years.

Kylie's 13th year also saw an exciting family holiday to Britain. As well as visiting her mother's relatives in Wales, Kylie took in the London sights of

"When you are 14 or 15 you are very possessive about clothes, especially if your little sister has them on"

Tower Bridge, Buckingham Palace, Trafalgar Square and Madame Tussaud's, vowing one day to return.

Furthering her interest in music, the teenager embraced pop. The first concert she attended was Culture Club in Melbourne. "I must have been about 14 and I thought I was a good version of Boy George –I had my hair in all the ribbons and plaits. I probably thought everyone was looking at me because my hair looked so fantastic, but I'm sure I looked just diabolical." She also had a huge crush on Adam Ant.

"I loved Adam. Those eyes. I still shudder at the name. He was so gorgeous."

"But then again, no doubt one member of The Partridge Family and one of The Osmonds also probably got a look in."

Having two girls in the house could have proved difficult, but generally Kylie got on well with her sister – that is, apart from the time Kylie returned to find Dannii wearing one of her dresses and a blazing row erupted. "When you are 14 or 15 you are very possessive about clothes, especially if your little sister has them on," laughs Kylie today.

But by now Dannii Minogue wasn't your average little sister. At the age of 11 the promising performer had secured an ongoing spot in a weekly TV variety show called *Young Talent Time* and had rapidly become a household name. One of Kylie's sibling duties was to forge Dannii's handwriting in answering the sackfuls of fan mail that poured in. "My sister was the famous one," says Kylie. "She was the one who was recognised in the street."

If Kylie was jealous she never showed it, although she admits to getting a little tired of introducing herself as "Dannii's sister." In fact she had other things on her mind. "I discovered boys and everything that goes with boys, and I realised you didn't have to go to school. I could just wag and smoke cigarettes all day. I wasn't really bad –I just did the normal things." Despite her rebellion, at 16 Kylie successfully completed her High School

Certificate and took on a job in a local video store.

Gainful employment proved uninspiring and, spurred on by Dannii's success, she convinced her parents to chaperone her to auditions across Australia. Fame was out there and she wanted to seize it with both hands.

Above: Kylie and her sister, Dannii

11

"In the first interview I had to do for *The Henderson Kids*, I remember saying, 'I don't want you to call me Dannii's sister. Call me Kylie.'"

"In the first interview I had to do for *The Henderson Kids*, I remember saying, 'I don't want you to call me Dannii's sister. Call me Kylie.'"

Along with Dannii, Kylie was among 1,000 teenagers who answered a newspaper advert for a new children's TV series called *The Henderson Kids*. The 16-year-old Kylie again beat her now famous sister, winning the role of tough 12-year-old, Charlotte Kernow. Filming started in October 1984 in selected rural locations outside Melbourne.

Although Kylie was delighted with her first role in six years, she was mortified at the prospect of dying her blonde hair red to get into character. "It was pretty shocking. I remember going to school and everyone staring at me and I had to tell them that I hadn't done it out of my own free will. I was so embarrassed."

Filming continued for the next seven months and Kylie became close to the other young actors on set, enjoying many late-night sleepovers and the added bonus of a modest wage packet. Between takes she amused herself duetting with one of her co-stars.

a guest appearance in *The Zoo Family* in which her childlike stature again helped her portray a girl nearly five years younger. This was quickly followed by a lead role in *Fame And Misfortune*, a six-part mini-series which saw the 17-year-old develop further in another challenging part. After coaching from onset tutors, Kylie returned to school to complete Year 12 a minor celebrity, with her hair mercifully back to blonde.

When Kylie left school she was uncertain of her future. She'd enjoyed the past year's television exposure but harboured dreams of marriage, children and running her own handicraft store, "selling things like scented drawer liners, essential oils, country gardening books, all sorts of knick-knacks." Alternatively, she was considering taking a

"It was during that time that I became more interested in singing because I always used to sing with another girl on the set, Nadine Garner. It was the first time I harmonised."

Right and below: Kylie's trademark style in the mid-Eighties

Alongside expanding her vocal talents, Kylie also tackled the media, giving her first newspaper interview in December, and learned how to stage-cry. "I was really nervous but found out I could do it. The scene worked really well. Now I can get to those emotional moments and I can express them," she said confidently.

Kylie's experience in *The Henderson Kids* led to

course in fashion, combining her interest in sewing and knitting with her talent for designing her own clothes.

Despite her obvious enjoyment of acting, these thoughts were still at the forefront of her mind when she attended a successful casting for a low-budget soap called *Neighbours* in January 1986.

Chapter 2: I Should Be So Lucky

"Jason and I are very good friends for sure…but as for romance, there's too much pressure on us to think about that"

NEIGHBOURS, A SQUEAKY-CLEAN suburban soap opera, was suffering from poor ratings and a changeover of TV networks. When an inquiry revealed the majority of viewers were teenage girls, the show's focus shifted towards youth plotlines, in an attempt to save it from being axed.

Consequently several new characters were created to enhance the show's pulling power, among them school friends Charlene Mitchell and Scott Robinson. Kylie began filming as the former in February 1986, joining her old colleague, Jason Donovan, as the latter.

The bountiful weekly pay-cheque changed Kylie's life enormously. "For a kid just out of school it was more than a paper round!" she recalls. "But my dad said, 'Don't feel guilty, you worked hard for it. Go out and buy something nice!' I guess that's when my love of shoes started…"

Aside from the inevitable shopping sprees, Kylie soon realised she had more than a passing attraction for Jason Donovan. Her main memory of him from Skyways was that he had been "really chubby with a bowl haircut". Now Jason, four days her junior and fellow Gemini, was 17 and definitely heart-throb material. The pair soon became boyfriend and girlfriend, and moved into the bungalow at the back of Jason's father's house.

The Australian audience first saw *Neighbours'* new girl in April 1986, and the character of Charlene aka 'Lenny' was so popular that Kylie's original 13-week contract was extended indefinitely. Kylie relished Charlene's bold nature, explaining the schoolgirl-cum-mechanic struck a chord with viewers "because she's an average teenager who has problems with her boyfriend and getting her career started. Charlene is really sensitive but doesn't show it. She's a bit of a rebel and they probably relate to that. While she has her problems, she will always come out on top."

As Charlene and Scott grew in public esteem and developed their own onscreen relationship, the suits at *Neighbours* felt that the actors' offscreen relationship should be kept secret. Charlene and Scott had many fans of the opposite sex who would be disappointed to discover their heroes weren't single. Additionally, the 'are-they-aren't-they' media speculation about the show's brightest stars was proving an effective promotional gimmick. So Kylie and Jason were forbidden to conduct their affair openly. They agreed, knowing their jobs were at stake, and *Neighbours'* ratings soared.

"Jason and I are very good friends for sure," said Kylie over and over again to the press. "But as for romance, there's too much pressure on us to think about that."

❤ ❤ ❤ ❤ ❤

Below and right: Kylie and her on-and-offscreen boyfriend, Jason Donovan

"Whenever I used to feel on top of the world, I would just open my mouth and sing, and not care too much about what came out. Let's face it, singing is a fun, happy thing to do."

Six months into the *Neighbours* epidemic, Kylie was asked to sing with her co-stars at a benefit concert for an Aussie Rules football team. She agreed, willingly taking to the stage at Melbourne's Festival Hall in front of 1,500 supporters and choosing her own song.

> **I** *knew the words to 'The Loco-Motion', the backing was simple and the band knew the song, so we raced out and gave an impromptu performance.*

Loving the limelight, Kylie then joined Dannii to sing Eurythmics and Aretha Franklin's 'Sisters Are Doin' It For Themselves' on *Young Talent Time*. Soon after she agreed to record a demo tape of 'The Loco-Motion' at Sing Sing studios, but thought little of it and continued her breakneck schedule on *Neighbours*.

During the next year Kylie was heavily involved in demanding publicity tours in support of the show. Each weekend it was normal for her to fly across Australia by helicopter to appear in shopping centres and nightclubs, signing autographs and fielding questions. Already the love story flourishing between Charlene and Scott was drawing millions of viewers. *Neighbours* was elevated to the teatime slot, fully recovered from its hiccup of the previous

year and fast becoming Australia's biggest soap.

Meanwhile, Kylie's demo of 'The Loco-Motion' (a Little Eva hit from 1962) had reached the offices of Mushroom Records and after some deliberation they signed the 18-year-old actress. The idea was to release a rerecorded version of the track in time to tie in with the TV event of the year – the wedding of Scott and Charlene.

Kylie and Jason were frequently mobbed by fans and police intervention was necessary at Sydney's Royal Easter Show, where they made an appearance. Days later the couple emerged triumphant from the *TV Week Logies*; Jason as Best New Talent and Kylie as Most Popular Australian Actress. "When it was announced I just went into shock," said Kylie. "Honestly, I didn't think I'd win. I'm really lucky going from school to a full-time job like this in a show which is so popular. It wasn't until somebody asked me what Logie I'd won that I realised how important it was for me."

Soon after, Kylie appeared at a televised anti-drugs concert, duetting on 'Sisters Are Doin' It For Themselves' with Dannii and Howard Jones' 'No One Is To Blame' with Jason. Her secondary career as a pop star looked promising.

The momentous occasion that was Charlene and Scott's wedding was aired in early July 1987 and predictably drew in the highest ratings in the history of Australian TV. Fans were glued to their screens as they watched Lenny float up the aisle to the sound of Angry Anderson's 'Suddenly', later a hit single in its own right. But for Kylie, the filming was far from emotional.

"I must have walked up and down that aisle 20 times while we were trying to capture the right

Below: Kylie as Charlene in *Neighbours*, a schoolgirl-cum-mechanic

Kylie

"Michael Hutchence made an effort to come over and say hi, which was good of him"

mood," she complained. "I'm sure it made a beautiful scene but I had to think of it as a day's work." At this time she also began to question her influence on her admirers. "It was really weird with the wedding. I'd have people coming up to me thinking that I was really getting married. People look up to you so much and I'm just a normal person and it's a bit frightening that they are all watching everything that you do."

The *Neighbours* union went down in history, having repercussions even for the matriarch of the soap many years later. "Did you know that Helen Daniels dies watching Scott and Charlene's wedding video?" said Kylie a decade later. "How cruel is that? That really pulls on the viewers' heartstrings doesn't it?"

Two weeks after the wedding, Kylie's debut single, 'The Loco-Motion', was released in Australia. It shot straight to the top of the charts, where it would stay for seven weeks (and would eventually become the biggest-selling Australian single of the Eighties). Kylie was at home with her family when she heard the news.

"A station in Melbourne used to play the Top Eight at 8 o'clock in the evening and the countdown had already started. Number five, not me. Number four, number three. Come number two, I thought, 'Oh, I'm not in it'. It did not cross my mind that I would be number one. And then the announcement said,

rocker with tight leather trousers and an intense gaze – was also present. Kylie was totally and utterly star-struck.

"I thoroughly enjoyed the *Countdown* awards," she said later. "I was worried that a lot of the famous big-time rock music people would look down on me as just a soapie star moving in on their area and zooming up the chart. But they were all really nice. Michael Hutchence made an effort to come over and say hi, which was good of him."

❤   ❤   ❤   ❤   ❤

Life as Kylie knew it evaporated as she ploughed into an endless flurry of promotion, overseen by Blamey and Mushroom Records. "You could lose yourself in all that publicity hype," she said. "I have seen what happens to people who can't and don't cope with the pressure. It's possible to lose what you have. That's when you have to keep yourself separate and not confuse your personality with all the publicity. I realised early on that when it's over, you only have yourself left."

Towards the end of 1987, Kylie took a fortnight off filming to cultivate her pop career in London. Fortuitously, Mushroom Records had ties with the English pop team, songwriters Mike Stock and Matt Aitken, and producer Peter Waterman, aka SAW. The trio were ridiculously successful with their conveyor-belt attitude to pop, proving they could make stars of normal folk. They scored dozens of hits with

Far left: Kylie and *Neighbours* co-star Jason Donovan and Peter O'Brien at the *Countdown Music Awards in July 1987* where she met Michael Hutchence for the first time

'Well, we've got a new entry this week, it's Kylie Minogue...' I just squealed! I couldn't believe it. ''

As the success of the single thundered on, she employed a manager, Terry Blamey. Later the trend of *Neighbours* pop stars continued with Jason Donovan, Craig McLachlan, Guy Pearce and Stefan Dennis following in Kylie's footsteps. But for the meantime the focus was on Kylie.

Now a household name, she was thrilled to join Australia's elite at as many celebrity functions as she could fit in her diary. In July 1987, sporting see-through platform shoes and white tights, Kylie attended the post-awards party of the *Countdown Music Awards* in Sydney. The lead singer of million-selling Aussie band INXS – a Jim Morrison-styled

Bananarama, Sinitta, Mel & Kim and Rick Astley, and several of their records had made the transition down under. Mushroom believed Kylie could fit their bill.

Somewhere along the line Kylie's visit wasn't properly communicated to SAW. She waited in vain for their call, finally arriving on their doorstep in desperation on her last day in England. Only then were the wheels put in motion to start the collaboration and as Kylie sat in reception nervously knitting away, the team churned out a song. The lyrics were based on a chance remark that the soap star was "lucky" to be in this position at all. When

Above and far right:
Kylie on and off camera at the
time of 'I Should Be So Lucky'

"I *have to keep pinching myself to believe it's all happening,"*

"I have to keep pinching myself to believe it's all happening," she said.

The single also reached number one in Germany, Israel, Switzerland and Finland, and was a substantial hit in America.

By now Kylie couldn't step outdoors without being hounded by the press. As well as the inevitable Kylie-haters sprouting up in the papers and on the radio, rumours were rife – speculating on her love life, her rivalry with Dannii, her weight. Some even suggested that it was not her voice on 'I Should Be So Lucky', but Rick Astley's sped up to twice its normal tempo.

"There was a time in the late Eighties when a lot of nasty stuff had been written about me in the press in Australia," she recalls. "I found that very hard to cope with – it was all about me being rubbish and annoying. We call it tall poppy syndrome – being a little too successful too quickly and then being cut down to size. I guess I hadn't proved myself and I ruffled a few feathers – along comes this blonde strumpet who hogs the number one position for weeks on end."

The most shocking claims were that the petite singer was anorexic. Journalists drew on Kylie's comments that she existed on just "fruit, prawns and water" and preferred being "skinny" to "curvy", creating a myth that she was at death's door in her refusal to eat. Concerned fans began to send takeaway meals to the Minogue family home and Kylie was furious.

Kylie was finally summoned into the recording booth, she sang the hastily scribbled words with only a basic bass and drum pattern as accompaniment. Hours later she was on the plane home, learning her lines for *Neighbours*.

Kylie couldn't have chosen a better environment in which to release 'I Should Be So Lucky' early in 1988. *Neighbours* was not only drawing millions of fans on home turf but it had also taken over British airwaves. The new year introduced a revised UK teatime slot, drawing ratings of between 15 and 20 million viewers every night. Charlene and Scott were now well-established figures for the British youth.

Thanks to her success with 'The Loco-Motion', Kylie's second single – released on PWL (Peter Waterman Limited) Records – raced up the charts in Australia. In Britain it took a little longer to gain momentum, but with the aid of a cheap'n'cheerful promo video featuring Kylie in a bubble bath, and the prime photo opportunity of meeting Princess Diana at Australia's bicentennial celebrations, soon it was also number one in the UK. 'I Should Be So Lucky' stayed in this position for the next six weeks and Kylie was beside herself.

"I *am lucky, lucky, lucky to live in a country which affords a young person the opportunity to have a go and make a success of herself."*

"Other people try to lose weight whereas I'm always trying to gain it. But that doesn't make me an anorexic. A reporter once called and said, 'Hi Kylie – I hear you're an anorexic'. When the call came I was just about to bite into this huge triple-layer sandwich. We all thought that was pretty funny."

Observations on Kylie's size continued to dog her and eventually she just accepted matters. "If I had my time again, I would ask for a penny every time I met someone and they said, 'Oh, you're so small!' Or every time I was pre-empted in an article with any one of those descriptions; pint-sized, elfin. But then I am the smallest person I know, so I can't blame people. It's not going to go away."

In the midst of all this unwanted attention, Kylie's health suffered both physically and mentally. She came close to a breakdown after unceremoniously bursting into tears during a recording session. "I was very tired and emotional when I broke down," she says. "I could not carry on.

"I had the whole world asking, 'Who is this girl?' I kept saying, 'I'm just a kid from a soapie and I've released a record. What do you want from me?'"

"I was so sick, I had to take a day off. It gave me a few minutes to stop and think about what the hell I was doing. There was just so much pressure from so many people. I was so concerned about doing the right thing for everybody else and trying to maintain my sanity at the same time, which I think I did, just. On a couple of occasions I didn't. I worked myself to the bone. I was anaemic half the time and ill. Working, working, working."

The pressure didn't let up and, when she returned to London in March 1988 to record more songs with SAW, it instead increased dramatically. Topless photos of Kylie taken on a Balinese beach with Jason Donovan instantly made the front pages of newspapers worldwide. The teenager did her best to take it all in her stride, continuing to deny any romance with her co-star and laughing it off. "I confess I got a bit of a shock when the pictures appeared. But I'm not ashamed of my body. I like sunbathing topless," she explained.

Alone in London, bar her manager and security guards, Kylie turned to her parents for comfort. "My father made me realise I wasn't superhuman and that I needed to take care of myself," she said. "My parents are fantastic, they're the stabilising influence in my life. It is very hard for me to comprehend what is happening to me at home in Australia, let alone here in Britain. But I know they are there, along with my sister Danielle and brother Brendan, and it is a great source of strength for me."

Kylie also angrily stood up to constant media allegations of being a manufactured product. "They call me things like plastic person and a bimbo. I am not stupid. If I was stupid I don't think I would have got this far." She revealed her personal favourite tabloid tale was *Is Kylie An Alien?* "The story was all about how if there was an alien life form then they would have certain features. And they decided to match up these features to mine. They used the topless photo of me on the front page and they were saying that these aliens would have elfin features and small breasts.

"Because I'm only young, and have lived such a short and normal life, they run out of things to say about me. I can't always ignore what they write, but I can say it's a lot of crap!" Joking aside, she was later to admit, "You can't touch the media. There's nothing you can do. And I remember feeling helpless about that."

Far left: The early media intrusion occasionally got to Kylie

Chapter 3: Things Can Only Get Better

"The era of puffball skirts — what a time to become famous!"

Three

THE KYLIE MINOGUE PHENOMENON continued with the release of her next single, 'Got To Be Certain'; another chirpy slice of bubblegum pop from the SAW hit factory which reached number two in the UK a fortnight before Kylie's 20th birthday, and number one in Australia. The following month the inevitable happened – Charlene finally bowed out of *Neighbours*.

"I thought my last day was going to be emotional and it was," said Kylie. "I bawled my eyes out. I cried because I knew when I walked out on Ramsay Street, it would be a hundred times more difficult to see my friends. I owe a hell of a lot to *Neighbours* and I will always remember that. OK, so it isn't *Gone With The Wind*, but it's very popular, and I'm proud to have been associated with it."

Jason aka Scott was soon to follow Kylie out of the show, with his own plans to record with SAW already taking shape. The couple moved to a small house in Richmond, Melbourne. Despite Kylie's departure from *Neighbours*, Mushroom Records had recognised the benefits of keeping their relationship secret and the pair continued to oblige, perhaps a little less willingly.

"Jason was like a school sweetheart," says Kylie of this time together. "We started out as actors, just happy to have a job in *Neighbours*, and saw our careers grow from there. We were like soulmates. No one really understood the pressure we were under, so we had a lot of shared experiences."

Kylie's debut album, *Kylie!* demanded of her a whirlwind three-month tour, and before she left Australia she was careful to present herself modestly to the press.

"There is obviously an ambitious streak in me but I do realise that I'm still very young and inexperienced. I have never written a song or acted in theatre or a big movie, so there is still lots to learn."

Touring the UK and most of Europe (France, Germany, Spain and Denmark) was a necessary part of the promotion for *Kylie!* and in public the singer savoured the chance to travel extensively. "The idea of this tour was great. I know it is hard work but what other girl of my age is lucky enough to go around the world?" she asked her fans. Soon, however, the cracks began to show. "Travelling is a strange thing. I love it because it means I get to lots of other countries and see different people and different cultures, and I hate it because it's such a hassle and keeps me away from my family and friends."

Privately Kylie was suffering dreadfully from a phobia of flying. "I would do anything rather than fly, it scares me to death," she confessed. "I look at the aircraft and wonder is this one going to stay up there? It never gets any better, and I never do any less flying. I don't know why I'm so scared. I suppose because one is so helpless, there's nothing you can do if anything goes wrong and it's an awful long way down..."

Kylie's hard work paid off as her album went straight to number one in Britain. The SAW single version of 'The Loco-Motion' followed swiftly behind, eventually achieving number two in the UK charts and an impressive number three in the US. By the end of July 1988, *Kylie!* had sold 330,000 copies in the UK alone. It also went Top 10 and beyond in

"At the moment, I'm just flowing with the tide, following whatever is on offer to me that I like."

Right and below: Kylie tries and fails to experiment with changing styles to escape from her girl-next-door image

Australia, New Zealand, Japan, Germany, Finland, Denmark, Switzerland, Norway and Israel.

"I can hardly believe it!" exclaimed Kylie. "The album just doesn't stop selling. It's all down to Stock, Aitken and Waterman. I'm just a beginner, they're the guys with all the experience. I love the songs they write for me." Tellingly she continued, "I'm not even sure what my musical style is. As I progress I hope to develop musically. I don't know what my future style will be but the one thing I do know is that it will keep on changing."

Below: Kylie in 1988

For a 20-year-old from the Melbourne suburbs, Kylie wasn't doing badly. The harshest criticism hadn't harmed her wholesome image as everybody's favourite girl-next-door and her British fan club alone had 25,000 members. It was estimated she became a millionairess by mid-1988 and was earning on average £10,000 for brief public appearances.

Initially she balked at the idea of linking herself to commercial merchandise, saying, "There have been offers from cosmetics and hair product firms that I have turned down. I am concentrating on music and developing my acting. I really do believe it

> "I don't know what my future style will be but the one thing I do know is that it will keep on changing."

should be one step at a time." Soon enough though, the benefits of sponsorship beckoned and Kylie signed a £1 million Japanese deal to endorse cars, electrical goods and phone cards. Two years later she would film an Australian advert for Coca-Cola.

America was next on the list of territories to conquer, and Kylie arrived there in August 1988. She quickly signed with an American agency and began to weigh up film scripts. "I'm considering doing a mini-series set in the Fifties called *The Silence Of Dean Maitland*. Dean is a priest and I play a young girl called Diane who has an affair with him. It is very heated," she said, stressing that she wished to move away from her 'safe' image, a residue from *Neighbours*. When asked her choice of leading man, she aimed high. "The guys I would like to work with would be Mel Gibson, River Phoenix or Michael Hutchence from the Australian band INXS."

But Kylie's cheerful appearance was deceptive. A fortnight or so into the American leg of her tour, she cancelled the rest of the trip and returned to Australia: exhausted, missing her home... and Jason. Her boyfriend's own pop career was looking extremely bright by September. His SAW debut single, 'Nothing Can Divide Us' had quickly climbed to number eight in the UK. Although the lovers were still supposed to be keeping their relationship a secret, Kylie took charge and revealed the truth in a magazine interview during this same month.

"I guess everyone knows we are going out together," she sighed. "It's just that we've never admitted it before. I don't mind people knowing about my career, but I don't see why I should share everything. It's good to have a little mystery in your life.

"We try to avoid anyone seeing us together and try to use different entrances and exits when we meet.

> "*If everyone knew about Jason and me, it would spoil the mystique.*"

"I tell everyone that I'm still living with my mum and dad. But I don't live there all the time. I miss being with Jason. That's one of the reasons I don't like going on tour for too long. I really miss him when we're apart."

Unfortunately for Jason, no one, including his girlfriend, told him about her revelations. Three days after the interview appeared in print, Jason was asked about Kylie on a live TV programme. After reciting his usual spiel of denial, Jason got the shock of his life when the TV host asked him if he hadn't read what Kylie had said in the magazine.

Reeling, the music producers and managers insisted Kylie and Jason lived down the events of the last few days by pretending nothing had ever happened and that Kylie's remarks had been a figment of the journalist's overactive imagination. Jason's official response soon surfaced.

"I don't want to get into a big row over this and therefore I won't offend the magazine and say they're wrong," he said. "But the fact is I see Kylie as a best friend and not a lover. I really enjoy her company and miss the fun we used to have together on *Neighbours*. But she just isn't my girlfriend. There is no one in my life right now."

This unhappy period in Kylie's life corresponded with an unpleasant incident where she discovered an intruder rifling through her drawers in her parents' house. Fortunately Kylie's screams frightened him off, but the unconfirmed rumours suggesting the prowler was a known rapist certainly didn't help the singer's delicate frame of mind.

The only thing to do was to bury herself in endless publicity, and with her latest single, 'Je Ne Sais Pas Pourquoi', a number two hit, Kylie took off for two dates in a Tokyo nightclub in November 1988. There she mimed in front of an audience of 300, somehow overcoming the embarrassment of the tape machine breaking down in the middle of her performance.

Putting the awkwardness of her magazine gaff aside, Kylie next joined Jason to record a Christmas duet, written by SAW – supposedly due to thousands of pre-orders for a single that did not yet exist. The continuing popularity of *Neighbours* and fascination in the lovers' private lives provided a guaranteed hit. Kylie and Jason assisted by putting in a series of personal appearances together, including a reunion with the *Neighbours* cast at December's Royal Command Performance in London. 'Especially For You' went to number two in Australia and was a major hit across Europe. It eventually reached number one in the UK in January 1989, having lost the coveted Christmas spot to Cliff Richard's 'Mistletoe And Wine'.

On the surface it seemed all was well

Above: Kylie on the set of an early video and, left, with Jason, pretending not to 'be together', at a celebrity party.

Far right: Kylie with co-star Charlie Schlatter promoting *The Delinquents*
Below: Kylie adopts a sassier image

musically, but underneath Kylie was unhappy with her lack of involvement in the recording of her first album. "I wanted my voice to come through and it doesn't," she said over the New Year. "I feel very removed from this album because I didn't have much say about it and it doesn't sound like me. They did what they thought they had to do to deliver a hit, but the album isn't me."

She was becoming more and more frustrated by the public's perception of her as a SAW / PWL puppet. "As for the idea that I am being somehow manipulated, all I can say is that I have been in a similar industry – television – for the last couple of years and I know how it works," she insisted.

> " I intend to stay in control – I will make my own decisions all the way. "

As 1989 commenced, Kylie vowed to take charge of her career. For starters she worked on a new, slightly more streetwise image to separate her from the 'girl-next-door'. Her revised sophistication came in tandem with her first major film role as Lola Lovell in *The Delinquents*.

Based on a novel by Criena Rohan, the film is set in conservative Fifties Australia and follows the lives of two star-crossed lovers, Brownie (played by Charlie Schlatter) and Lola, as they rebel against their elders and embark on a life of petty crime.

Having previously been offered scores of scripts she described as "pretty crummy" Kylie jumped at the chance to work on a major movie, to be produced by Mike Wilcox and Alex Cutler for Village Roadshow, a subsidiary of Warner. Filming began in mid-April in Maryborough, a sleepy town in Queensland.

"It's a bit nerve-racking because there are a lot of expectations on me," Kylie admitted. "Even if I do a good job it'll be hung on me anyway. The question the press keep asking is, 'How are the fans going to react to me changing from sweet, innocent squeaky-clean Kylie to this girl that has sex and smokes?' I'm trying to get it through to them that it's not me. I'm acting and it's just me keeping moving as an actress."

Over the next two months Kylie gave an enthusiastic and committed performance as Lola and enjoyed a newfound respect from her colleagues. "The whole experience has been fun and the crew have been fantastic, especially in the very beginning because I was nervous," she said. "It was, after all, my film debut, and you only get one chance at it."

The question of Lola's upfront sexuality was one that Kylie chose to underplay, emphasising that the role in no way reflected her personal life. She described the film as, "tasteful – I wouldn't have let it through if it wasn't," then, "I've had a great family life and haven't had the sort of problems she encountered. Lola went through an abortion, moved out of home and was constantly on the run from the cops. I just tried to imagine what it would have felt like, but couldn't draw on any past experiences."

Ultimately the Australian film suffered from becoming too Americanised due to the demands made by a US production company. Despite its unintentional corniness, teenagers loved it and *The Delinquents* did well in Britain and Australia, but ironically sank without trace in America, and was soon released on video. Kylie stood by her movie.

"I'm proud of the film, I really am. If people hate it and it's a flop, well, that's all there is to it. But I worked hard and really looked inside myself for new emotions. The film will always be a very special memory for me."

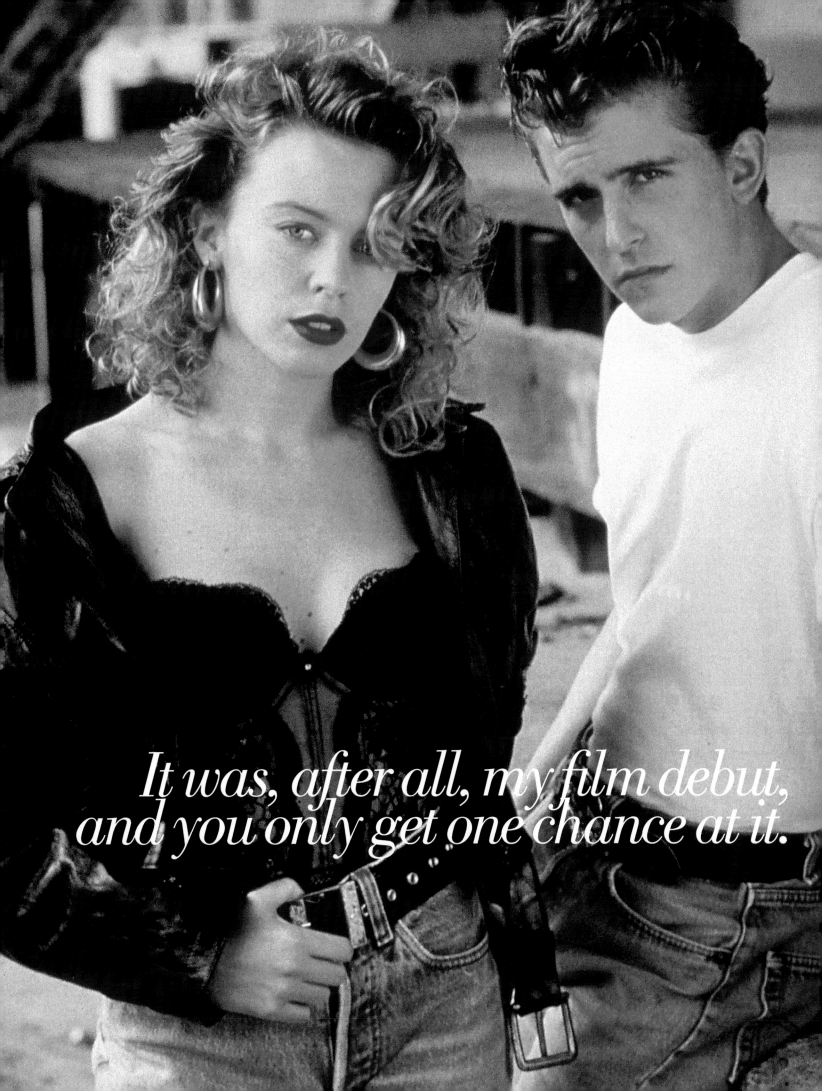

It was, after all, my film debut, and you only get one chance at it.

Chapter 4: Some Kind Of Bliss

"I'm going to have to act like I'm an adult and have no excuses to act like a kid."

BEFORE FILMING OF *THE DELINQUENTS* concluded in late June 1989, Kylie's musical career had bubbled away with the release of 'Hand On Your Heart', her sixth single and third UK number one. It was also a big hit in Germany, whose charts confirmed that since January 1988 Kylie had constantly had at least one single in the Top 40. Japan was another territory she dominated and in March 1989 she witnessed no less than five of her singles appearing in that country's Top 40 at the same time – 'I Should Be So Lucky' (number 31), 'The Loco-Motion' (27), 'It's No Secret' (4), Especially For You' (3) and 'Turn It Into Love' (1) – the latter a Japanese release on Alfa Records, which held on to its top position for an incredible 10 weeks.

Meanwhile the singer celebrated her 21st birthday in high style, at a $100,000 party attended by nearly 200 friends.

"My life has changed drastically. It has made me a lot tougher and a lot more business wise."

Kylie quipped of her mature status, "I'm going to have to act like I'm an adult and have no excuses to act like a kid."

Indeed, Kylie's adult transformation was apparent in many ways. As befitted a pop star of the time, she became a willing spokeswoman for the perils of global warming. "I think Green issues are very, very important and everyone should get involved wherever they can and take notice of the problems," she said. "I do what I can to help and one day I would really like a shop full of Green products. It would make sense to stop products that damage the environment." Apparently Kylie also refused to handle everyday plastics which couldn't be broken down naturally.

Having tentatively toyed with a sexier image than presented by the early days with SAW and the

aftermath of *Neighbours*, Kylie now became deeply involved with the projection of her public persona. She employed a full-time stylist, Nicole Bonython. "In the last few months, people have noticed my change in style – that's fantastic," said Kylie. "It was a specific move, done on purpose. I'm really comfortable with the image I project now."

This move towards overseeing her appearance also prompted the singer to take stock of her career direction. She spoke out about the pressure to follow *The Delinquents* with a major Hollywood role. "I don't think there is any rush for me to get to America and make films. I don't think it's a big deal. Major movies are being made all the time in other countries, particularly in Australia and Britain."

Encouraged by her accountant father, Kylie's shrewd business sense was founded at this time.

"I try to keep my eyes on everything. That's why I have a manager and people to do things for me, because some things I just don't have time to do myself. It has taken me quite a while to be able to do that."

In the summer of 1989, Kylie's fast-developing need for control overspilled into a court case with *Neighbours* producers Grundy's. She attempted to halt the release of a video entitled *Scott And Charlene: A Love Story*, which was compiled without her permission and paid her no fee. Kylie felt the product was a blatant cash-in on her popularity since leaving the soap and, more importantly, unnecessarily linked her to a previous incarnation in the eyes of the public. The judgement however ruled that as the programme had unequivocally launched

Far left and below: Kylie on the set of 'Hand On Your Heart'

Above: Kylie in the late Eighties

As Kylie returned to London to record her second album with SAW, she set about finding an apartment she could call home. It seemed that, for the foreseeable future, her work would be permanently overseas.

Arriving at the Vine Yard studios in August, Kylie's new business confidence initially inspired her to concern herself more in the production of her material. SAW disagreed and once again the singer's actual input was minimal. Privately frustrated, in public she stood by her music team.

"At the start, I didn't know much about SAW or how the music industry operated," she said. "Now I've got more knowledge and people expect me to leave them. I haven't written my own songs yet but my answer to people who criticise me for not doing that is, hey, when I'm ready. SAW are good at doing that and I must be good at bringing it across in a way people can relate to and enjoy. We cop a lot of flak because we're commercial but you have to have a lot of talent to be commercial."

It seemed despite her leanings towards greater artistic involvement, the star was grateful for her backing and determined not to rest on her laurels. "You can never sit back and relax and think, 'Oh right I've made it, I don't have to work as hard any more,' because, as Mike Stock's always saying to me, you're only as good your last record," she said. "The public are fickle and they could change their minds at any time. I guess the main thing is to enjoy being successful while it's happening." Years later she was to comment on the SAW recording process, "You see a song for the first time, and 20 minutes later the red light goes on and you sing. Professional job, just like reading from a script for a soap."

The album, entitled *Enjoy Yourself*, and accompanying housey single, 'Wouldn't Change A Thing', were predictably popular. Repeating the tone and image from *Kylie!*, they went to number one and two in the UK charts respectively. Elsewhere the story was much the same, as *Enjoy Yourself* went Top 10 in Australia, Belgium, Norway, Japan, Greece and number one in Hong Kong. But the artistic differences were growing and in interviews Kylie hinted her next project would be more of a challenge.

"With *Enjoy Yourself*, I said to SAW, 'I want to be able to sing on it'," she said. "And yeah, I am clouded by computers a lot of the time, but that's pop music. And I don't want to just drop pop music. I like it. *Enjoy Yourself* is a step in the right direction and with the next one I want to take a leap, because I've got new confidence in myself and I think I'll have something more to offer."

Kylie's career, Grundy's were within their rights to profit from the character of Charlene.

Kylie was furious. "I spent a lot of time getting away from Charlene. I don't want this sort of thing stuck on the shelves forever. I'm sure there are a lot of people who say, '*Neighbours* has made what you are.' Well, it hasn't. It's exploitation."

❤ ❤ ❤ ❤ ❤

"London has come to be my second home, but it has taken some time to get used to it. I've been coming here for some time and only now am I relaxed here. For quite a while I was pretty lonely."

❤ ❤ ❤ ❤ ❤

To promote her new album, Kylie went on the road with the Disco In Dreams roadshow. She would sing live to back-up tapes, supported by four dancers. Her first major concerts took place in Japan, which is where she collided once again with Michael Hutchence. Her life changed irrevocably.

After their first meeting two years previously, Kylie had run into Michael briefly when Jason took her to see his favourite band, INXS, play in Melbourne. This third time Kylie was on her own and Michael, then a Hong Kong resident, made his move. After being spotted sight-seeing around town together, reports came in that the couple were sharing a hotel room.

It has to be said that the possibility of the hard-edged, raunchy rock star, eight years Kylie's senior, taking a genuine interest in the bouncy young SAW artist was highly implausible; especially as Michael had made several derogatory comments about her in the press. But opposites really did attract and the pair arranged to meet after Kylie's touring commitments ended.

Passionately smitten with her new lover, Kylie was left with the problem of splitting up with Jason. This she dealt with in a long-distance phone call, made all the worse by the identity of his usurper. "I was still in love with Kylie and what made it even harder was that she went off with the man I wanted to be," Jason admitted many years later.

A second cruel irony was the timing of the break-up, which corresponded exactly with the UK showing of the *Neighbours* wedding of Scott and Charlene, attracting some 20 million viewers. But Kylie was determined to put her past behind her and reinvention was on the cards.

Together the couple returned to Sydney, where Michael was due to record *X*, the follow-up to the hugely successful INXS album, *Kick*. He wasted no time in embroiling Kylie in his social scene; one very much entwined with artists of all genres including

Above: Kylie attends the Australian premiere of *The Delinquents* in late 1989, accompanied by her new lover, Michael Hutchence

> 66 *I was tied down to a childhood relationship with Jason and once I got out of that, my world opened up* 99

So Kylie was free to go with Michael. At least this time around SAW had no say in whether she should keep her relationship under wraps – moreover the publicity generated by the affair had an extremely positive effect on her image. Suddenly Kylie had street cred.

"Michael's different from what people would expect," she told journalists rapt by this romance made in media heaven. "I'm sure people look at me and think I'm just two-dimensional and you can't imagine what it would be like to get beyond that. And Michael, he's really impressive. He's really deep sometimes. He has this label as the wild man of rock, but he's so many other things – he's incredibly charismatic."

music, film and fashion, but also one with a substantial dose of sex, drugs and rock'n'roll.

Michael's endorsement of Kylie secured her acceptance into this crowd. The experimentation was twofold. "He opened my eyes to a completely different world and I think I did the same for him," she explains. "He'd travelled down a lot of roads and to then start dating a naïve 21-year-old was a real eye-opener for him. He thought he knew everything about the world and then he met me and saw this little creature who was learning something every day. He used to say it was almost frightening watching me learn and grow up in front of him."

Michael made no secret of his unhealthy habits and Kylie unwisely allowed herself to be

"I'm all for kids not taking drugs. But I don't want to say to them you should never try anything. You have to experience something to have a view on it"

Top: Kylie attends a party for
The Delinquents
Right: With Michael Hutchence

quoted at this time as saying drug use "can be fun and it can be dangerous. I'm all for kids not taking drugs. But I don't want to say to them you should never try anything. You have to experience something to have a view on it." Unsurprisingly the reaction in the press prompted a swift retraction whereby Kylie stated she simply hadn't wanted to appear to "preach" to her fans.

In December Kylie made a brief return to the UK for the world premiere of *The Delinquents* and the SAW recording session for their remake of the Band Aid classic, 'Do They Know It's Christmas?' The song featured their entire stable of stars performing as Band Aid II and proceeds went to charity. Kylie's latest single, 'Never Too Late', had reached number four the previous month and her high profile helped guarantee a Christmas number one – alongside her ex-boyfriend, Jason Donovan.

Soon enough Kylie returned victorious to Sydney for the Australian premiere of *The Delinquents*, which she proudly attended with Michael by her side. Named 'Woman Of The Decade' by fellow Australian Clive James in his BBC comedy *Review Of The Decade*, Kylie was on top of the world. She was number one in the charts, her movie was playing to enthusiastic audiences all over the world and a new romance was blossoming as the Nineties began.

A new romance was blossoming as the Nineties began

Chapter 5: Dangerous Game

"Michael Hutchence told me when performing to imagine I was wearing an ego jacket for protection.
Then, if you say or do something silly, it's just the person in the jacket."

AS IF KYLIE'S LATE 1989 CHART PRESENCE wasn't enough, in January 1990 she released the ballad 'Tears On My Pillow' (a remake of Little Anthony & The Imperials' 1958 hit) taken from *The Delinquents'* soundtrack. Predictably the song shot to number one, aided by the triumphant Disco In Dreams Tour.

Kylie next took her roadshow to Australia, this time with a live backing band. Her first proper all-live dates were launched with a discreet gig under the name of The Singing Budgies, harking back to Kylie's old and much-detested nickname. "It will be a great challenge," said Kylie before the event. "It is a risk because it's putting myself out to be either raised up or thrown sticks at, but that's what this whole business is about. "

As the world wondered what Kylie would do next, she too was a little uncertain. Towards the end of 1989 SAW had toyed with the idea of writing a musical for her, which would also possibly star Jason Donovan, but this never transpired. Kylie instead pondered the merits of working on another film, preferably a comedy, but her wild months with Michael inspired her to concentrate on music.

Apart from 'I Should Be So Lucky' and 'The Loco-Motion' (which had reached number 28 and three respectively in the US charts), Kylie had met with nonchalance from America, traditionally a tough nut to crack as a pop star. Setting her sights on this market, Kylie arrived in Los Angeles to work with some respected American dance producers. For the first time Kylie was allowed to co-write her tracks and four of these songs would appear on her next album.

"It's pretty scary putting yourself up there
but you'll never learn if you never take the plunge."

She needn't have worried as the tour was a great success. Mid-way through she helped organise an extravagant 30th birthday party for Michael and 200 guests, including several well-known showbiz faces. Around this time a change in Kylie's appearance inspired Michael to write a song for her, to be included on INXS' next album, *X*. "Kylie dyed her hair this colour she called suicide blonde," Michael later recalled. "She said, 'I'm going to go suicide blonde today.' I think she was thinking of people like Marilyn Monroe and I thought it was a good name, especially as Madonna was big at the time." That autumn 'Suicide Blonde' became one of INXS' biggest transatlantic hits to date.

"The best way to describe my American work is as a collaboration," she enthused. "That's something I haven't done before and it was great. It's just like being given free rein to say what I want to say and how I want to say it. I learnt a lot from those guys and they were interested in what I had to say. With SAW songs, I heard them the day I recorded them, sometimes two songs in a day. But to work on a song, demo it and live with it for a while is bliss."

Among Kylie's new songs was 'Count The Days', dedicated to Michael. "That's about being away from each other because it's obviously difficult for us to match up – we're both so busy."

Immediately after finishing work in the States, Kylie flew to Britain to continue promotion of *Enjoy Yourself*. Her concerts were already completely sold-out. Thousands of British fans were thrilled to see a super-fit Kylie dance energetically through her show in a number of revealing sequinned outfits, a stringent fitness routine and vegetarian diet paying off many times over. Kylie was especially pleased as she had forbidden her mentors at SAW to see her plans for the show, undertaking the employment of choreographers and stylists herself in utmost secrecy.

The tour wound up in Bangkok in May, where the closing celebrations doubled as a 22nd birthday party for Kylie. Here she was reunited with Michael, who presented her with a diamond ring.

> "People try to put you down
> and say,
> 'You're just manufactured, you're a puppet.'
> If I was a manufactured puppet I wouldn't be able to sit in this room
> talking without someone's hand up my back,
> moving my mouth for me."

Never one to bow out of the public eye, as Kylie finished her tour to promote her last album she simultaneously released a single to introduce the next; *Rhythm Of Love*. The non-American tracks on the album, written by SAW, retained the harder, clubby sound of Kylie's recent singles, and although the cover shot was still pretty clean-cut, the content suggested the singer had moved on somewhat. 'Better The Devil You Know' was an up-tempo dance track, stylistically far removed from her previous material and an instant hit, achieving number two in the British charts (Kylie's hopes for American recognition still sadly unrealised). It featured in both the movie soundtrack for *If Looks Could Kill* and Kylie's Australian Coca-Cola advert later in 1990.

Behind the success lay a battle saga. Since becoming more business-minded when she'd turned 21, Kylie had worked to take charge of her image, including which photos were released and how she appeared in her videos. This was against the wishes of SAW, who fought to retain the cheesy, safe girl-next-door persona. But with Michael's rock music

credibility behind her, Kylie was not going to lose this power struggle, especially as she was far and away SAW's biggest star.

Kylie's control of her looks expanded into gaining final veto over which songs made it onto her albums. With 'Better The Devil You Know' she was unhappy with SAW's original version and demanded that it was remixed to suit the sexy athleticism she would project in the accompanying video – of which SAW also disapproved. It worked wonders and Kylie's music was actually played for the first time in the hippest clubs.

Kylie and Michael moved to London in June 1990, to complete work on their respective albums. Although both lives revolved around the music industry, their involvement didn't directly affect their work. "Michael encourages me to be myself, to go after my dreams, to go for what I want," said Kylie. "He gives me confidence. We both do our own thing with work. For too long my relationships were mixed in with work and I really didn't know where the line was. Now I'm in a position where I can step back and say this is work, this is my relationship."

Over the summer months they would jet set between their homes in London, Sydney, Hong Kong and France, leading a glitzy showbiz lifestyle of parties and pleasure. "Michael was such an amazingly smart, well-read, wild, poetic man," she later recalled. "It was very intense and wonderful and it drove my manager crazy, because Michael and I used to meet all over the place. I used to get my manager to shimmy things along so I could go to Frankfurt one weekend, then fly off to Hong Kong..."

During this time Michael was famously quoted as saying that his favourite hobby was "corrupting Kylie". Alongside speculation on the couple's intake of drugs, rumours flew that they had installed an S&M dungeon in their basement, they'd had sex on a plane with the Australian prime minister sitting nearby, and that she kept handcuffs in her handbag. Kylie denied the first charge and commented on the latter: "That story will follow me around forever. Everyone looks so unconvinced when I explain this.

"I had this little leather pouch with handcuffs as the handle. I was travelling to Monte Carlo from Heathrow, so I put the small handbag into a larger carrier bag. It never crossed my mind that they would be construed as a dangerous item. I put the bag through the X-ray machine and they took them off me and I wasn't allowed to collect them until the other end – in case I tried to handcuff someone to the plane or whatever..."

Image-wise, stories like these and Kylie's recent changes in appearance and music transformed her into an incarnation popularly known as 'SexKylie'. But Kylie's lips were sealed on the matter of her private time with Michael. "He was a wonderful teacher and lover. But it wasn't just sex he taught me. We'd all be very lucky if we could experience a man as charismatic as Michael."

Although Kylie's Seventies tribute, 'Step Back In Time', the second single to be released from *Rhythm Of Love*, went straight to number four in the charts, the album itself was slightly less well-received, achieving number nine in the UK and number 10 in Australia. America was again uninterested despite Kylie's concerted efforts to toughen-up her act.

Kylie didn't really mind. "The last year has been so fulfilling and personally great, not just work-wise," she said. "People are taking me a lot more seriously now. There's been a general change towards me everywhere and it's definitely for the better. I feel more solid, I feel like I've finally made it. For a one-hit wonder, I've been here for a long time."

In February 1991 Kylie was back on the road in promotion for *Rhythm Of Love*, starting in Perth. In the countries where it counted, her popularity was still strong and the tour was launched with the news that her latest single, the Hi-NRG 'What Do I Have To Do?', had reached number six in the UK. Remixed from the original album version, the single made waves within the media due to its full-on video. Kylie defended her latest look by saying she aspired to be "all-out glam... as many movie stars as possible; Sophia Loren, Brigitte Bardot, Elizabeth Taylor..."

While all was good on the work front, Kylie's private life wasn't as peachy. Having experienced a whirlwind 18 months with Michael Hutchence, finally his excessive lifestyle got the better of her and the couple split up. Michael's casual infidelities were cited as the cause and soon after he was publicly stepping out with supermodel Helena Christensen. Kylie was devastated but knew the relationship had become unhealthy.

"I was so hurt with the break-up because I was very much in love with him," she recalls. "I spent a good part of the time crying my heart out. There were days when I just wanted to stay in bed." To this day Kylie describes her romance with Michael as a critical turning point for her and refers to him as one of the great loves of her life.

Before the year was out the pair had recovered a platonic friendship and would occasionally be seen deep in conversation at INXS parties. But for now Kylie threw herself into a brand new affair with a South African former model called Zane O'Donnell, who had appeared in two of her music videos. After her tour Kylie and Zane settled in London and surrounded themselves with a whole new crowd based around the city's elite nightlife.

Perhaps as a result of the break-up with Michael, Kylie needed to let her hair down. "I'm not addicted in any way to drink, cigarettes or anything like that but I very much need interaction with people," she said. "I need to be enticed and stimulated and not be bored." Later she was to admit of this period: "I was out of control for a while. I was rebelling against everything I couldn't do before. I had to get it out of my system."

In June 1991, Kylie's single 'Shocked' charted at number six in the UK. Notably it was the first of her PWL releases not to be mixed by the

Below: By the early Nineties Kylie was opting for an all-out sex kitten look

Above: Kylie on the set of the video for 'Word Is Out'
Right: In John Galliano's G-string, frilly bra and fishnet stockings

usual team, instead re-worked by DNA (best known for their dance remix of Suzanne Vega's 'Tom's Diner'). The British music industry bible *Music Week* announced that the 23-year-old singer was "the only act in the history of British pop music to have their first 13 releases all go Top 10". It was quite an achievement for a little girl from Oz. Unhappily for her music producers, the little girl had just grown up.

The recording of Kylie's fourth album for SAW was fraught with tension. Although not contracted to do so, Kylie's manager encouraged her to resume the association one last time as it had obvious financial benefits. Kylie insisted on co-writing the majority of the tracks with Mike Stock (Matt Aitken had left the company earlier that year). The two did not often see eye-to-eye, coming from completely different schools of thought and with drastically different levels of experience. Gaps were filled with other SAW songs Kylie had recorded but not included on her previous albums.

Still, Kylie was pleased with the result, named *Let's Get To It*. Musically she had taken on a new direction, citing R&B, soul and swing references, and this was reflected by the Sixties bouffant hairstyle she adopted on the album's cover. Kylie claimed it was her favourite work so far but the public were not quite as convinced, and for the first time she saw her chart positions slide – the album reached number 15 in the UK and number 17 in Australia, and the first single lifted, 'Word Is Out', only came in at number 16. Still respectable, but not quite up to Kylie's usual Top 10 standards.

If the reviews were anything to go by ("an album of greater subtlety and depth than could ever have been imagined," said *Music Week*), it now seemed Kylie was appealing more to adults than teenagers – unfortunately for her they bought less records.

Even so, audiences could always be fooled. Intriguingly, a version of 'I Guess I Like It Like That' was released in advance of its parent album, *Let's Get To It*, on a white-label 12" under the pseudonym of Angel K. It soon became a firm club favourite, and was reissued in the mainstream by PWL with the new title, 'Keep On Pumpin' It', credited to The Visionmasters & Tony King Featuring Kylie Minogue. Minus any promotion whatsoever, not even a photograph on the cover sleeve, the single still managed to achieve number 49 in the UK charts – proving there was no holding the girl down. Shortly afterwards, another anonymous Angel K release appeared, again aimed at clubbers. 'Do You Dare' was less successful and was later recycled in 1992 as a B-side.

Still touring, Kylie hit Europe, where her choice of costumes brought more attention than her music. She had decided to work with the English designer John Galliano, and he had produced a series of tantalising outfits guaranteeing freedom of movement – and maximum exposure. "John Galliano is an absolute genius," Kylie proclaimed. "He came up with a G-string, a frilly bra and fishnet stockings that were totally outrageous. "

> " *But it so perfectly reflected what I was thinking at the time, it was frightening.* "

Kylie had wanted something that would be remembered for a long while after the event and the overt, garish sexuality suggested by her onstage attire certainly attracted press attention. Most of all she was compared to Madonna, not necessarily a bad thing as far as Kylie was concerned. "Madonna has definitely influenced me," she said. "She seems a very strong woman, continually breaking new ground. But I'm not trying to imitate Madonna. I'm continuing to develop my own style."

Most of all she was compared to Madonna

Chapter 6: Should I Stay Or Should I Go

> ❝I *think they lost the plot for a while and I told them that*❞

AFTER THE RELEASE OF *LET'S GET TO IT* the inevitable happened. Having changed so radically in both style and approach over the last few years, Kylie was virtually unrecognisable from the fluffy, starry-eyed teenager who had signed with PWL. The relationship no longer satisfied either party, so the singer parted company with her label and songwriting team.

"I think they lost the plot for a while and I told them that," Kylie revealed candidly. "Four years ago when they were really big, they had new sounds and they were ahead of their time. They've been doing so many songs and I don't know how long they can keep doing it well. People get jaded."

and 'What Kind Of Fool (Heard It All Before)' reached number 14: all respectable chart places.

Predictably, in November 1992 PWL cashed in for the last time on Kylie, releasing her *Greatest Hits* album, accompanied by a video collection. It featured her incredible run of 18 UK hits, all but three of which had attained Top 10 status. There were two new tracks on the album, including a cover of Kool & The Gang's 'Celebration' from 1980. The latter – one of Kylie's favourite songs – only managed number 20, but the album itself easily topped the charts. If Kylie was disillusioned, even she couldn't argue it was a truly impressive CV of her work with SAW.

❤   ❤   ❤   ❤   ❤

> ❝*They find a formula that works and stick to it. I can't do that. I've played safe for too long.*❞

As far as the public was concerned, little changed immediately. Throughout 1992 it was business as usual, with singles released from the album in standard succession. 'If You Were With Me Now' was Kylie's second romantically-themed duet, this time with respected American singer Keith Washington, and went to number four in the UK. Although both singers received joint co-writing credits with Mike Stock and Pete Waterman, they didn't actually meet until filming the accompanying video in London, having previously recorded their respective vocals separately.

Next Kylie's update of Chairmen Of The Board's 1970 UK hit, 'Give Me Just A Little More Time', achieved number two and was also used in an advert for Accurist watches. A remix of 'Finer Feelings' by Brothers In Rhythm went to number 11,

On a personal note 1992 was a quiet year for Kylie, apart from the obligatory promotion for her final PWL output. Having bought an apartment in Paris, she spent quality time away from the limelight, living with Zane in France. Towards the end of the year the couple returned to London, where Kylie had also purchased a base.

Situated on the sixth floor, Kylie's new Chelsea home was spacious and minimalist in style – the majority of the furnishings and decorations a stark white. "You would never know it's my place," she was to comment. "There's no indication of it being my place whatsoever."

Kylie fully embraced her adopted English lifestyle, after making some celebrity adjustments. She recalls, "I remember when I moved to London years ago, it took me ages to get a cleaner because I had that attitude that you can't have something that someone else doesn't, and you really shouldn't have someone clean up after you.

Far left: Kylie receives a kiss in the video for 'What Kind Of Fool (Heard It All Before)' and, below, hams it up in the video for 'Give Me Just A Little More Time'

Right: Kylie overcomes the challenge
of playing pool in high heels

"I do ordinary things. I go down to Europa and walk home with my shopping bags, I go to the movies... "

"**P**eople say to me, 'Don't you have a bodyguard?' And I'm like, pur-lease! It's a very Australian thing, I think."

Always an Aussie girl at heart, eventually Kylie began to think and act like an honorary Brit. To this day she enjoys going to the pub, playing snooker, backgammon and table tennis, eating chips and apple crumble, and catches a black cab wherever she goes.

"I've lived in London for years and, if I'm away, I really miss the place," she says today. "It's very much home and I always look forward to the moment when I get into a London cab and see a red double-decker bus go by."

Perhaps the most significant move for Kylie in 1992 was meeting and working with one of her all-time favourite idols, the artist known at that time as Prince. Back in 1989 she had revealed, "The day I meet Prince, my life will be complete. I think we'd make a great pair. He's an interesting person and the only artist I really admire as a fan. It's funny – he revolts some people but others think he's sex on a stick."

When quizzed on her favourite singers, Kylie had always made it painfully clear that she was desperate to link her name to his, in a musical sense

at least. "I'd love to work with him, he's my all-time hero. If Prince wanted to work with me, he'd obviously want to put his brilliance into what I do and God, I'd want that too. You think I'm going to say no?" A couple of years later she finally met him backstage after one of his London shows. The equally diminutive pop star was impressed with her enthusiasm and invited her to join him in the studio while he was still in town.

Although this was Kylie's dream come true, she misunderstood the nature of his working methods, believing he would create a song for her on the spot à la SAW. She arrived unprepared to sing and without so much as a lyric sheet. "There were a few jokes flying around," she later admitted. "I don't think he knew much about me, or at least he didn't let on. But he did mention one quote that I said some time back, about him being sex on a stick. I think I feigned ignorance, as if I didn't know what he was talking about. Which he probably saw straight through."

All was not lost however, and Prince suggested Kylie should visit him at his famous Paisley Park studio in Minneapolis the next time she was in America. Unfazed, Kylie took up the challenge, actually staying a few days and getting to know him personally as well as professionally. Together they worked on a track called 'Baby Doll', for which Kylie wrote the words and Prince provided the music. "I got to know something of Prince and he is a fairly reserved character," she teased eager journalists. "What I know about him I like and he's fine. He's a little weird but I'd be disappointed if he wasn't."

And was there any more to the musicians' relationship than work? "I didn't have a romance with him, we just hung out. I went to Paisley Park but I didn't go *there*...

"I think he's always a bit on the fresh side," she confided. "But who wants to be on that list? You think, hang on, I wonder how many other girls have been lured to Minneapolis? If that's what he enjoys, fine, but I'm interested in him and his music, nothing else."

While Kylie enjoyed the thrill of working with her hero, she debated what to do now she had left the confines of SAW and PWL. In 1993 she was initially unsure of her public standing sans recording contract, but gradually became aware of a previously untargeted pocket of fans. Oblivious over the years, Kylie had become a massive gay icon.

It was hardly surprising that the pop diva with a saucy sense of humour, outrageous outfits and dance music to match would attract an entire generation of gay fans. It all started right at the beginning, when 'I Should Be So Lucky' was released back in 1988. A gay pub, The Albury in Sydney, began to stage special Kylie Nights, where drag queens would mime to her music. Kylie wasn't told about this at the time as her management was concerned she wouldn't understand or appreciate her appeal, and perhaps do more harm than good in responding.

Five years later Kylie's gay fans were too numerous and vociferous to be ignored.

"What I love most about my gay audience is that the partnership we have happened very naturally," she says today. "I don't think the Pink Pound was even a term back in the Eighties. Today so many acts are marketed towards that audience; there's nothing wrong with that, but I try to market towards all demographics. In truth, with my gay audience, it happened before I knew about it."

Kylie finally came face to face with her 6' doppelgangers in another Australian club; Three Faces in Melbourne. "I remember I was blown away when I heard about the Kylie Show. I'd never seen anyone impersonating me, I was screaming my head

off! I laughed and laughed and laughed. One of them in particular, Millie Minogue, looked so much more like me than I did because I was kind of on the natural side. She was, you know, working everything. I feel I paled in comparison..."

As a result Kylie fully embraced the culture and appeared at many shows over the years, including a headlining appearance at the party following Sydney's annual Gay and Lesbian Mardi Gras parade in mid-1994. Kylie performed 'What Do I Have To Do?' clad in a miniscule pink tutu and supported by various drag queens in similar attire. "It was quite moving," she later commented. "I felt very touched at having such an appreciative crowd and just to be able to have the opportunity to say thank you."

Below: Ever conscious of her gay following, Kylie appeared at Gay Pride at Clapham Common in 1996

> "I've had a lot of support from the gay community."

Chapter 7: Falling

> *"I'm like, Bam! Bam! Bam!*
> *The film crew are like, 'She didn't even blink.*
> *Even Mel Gibson blinks when he fires his gun...'"*

IN THE SPRING OF 1993, KYLIE'S CAREER TOOK another turn as she wiped the slate clean and signed a fresh multi-million pound deal with trendy English dance label, deConstruction, a BMG subsidiary best known for its success with Mike Pickering's M People. The deal covered Kylie's music worldwide, with the exception of America, where she signed to Imago records, and Australia, where she remained with Mushroom. The rumours went that she was working with St. Etienne's Pete Wiggs and Bob Stanley on new material, but the truth was nothing would emerge for the next 18 months.

Still, Kylie was excited with her new musical home. "deConstruction have a brilliant reputation to uphold. So I'm kind of relying on their reputation rather than my own," she added tellingly.

Most of Kylie's 25th year passed quietly as she became used to working with some new faces, including deConstruction's own hit makers, production duo Brothers In Rhythm (Steve Anderson and David Seaman). Unfortunately her personal life didn't work out quite so well, as her relationship with Zane O'Donnell, which had been unstable of late, disintegrated towards the end of the year. In public at least, Kylie didn't seem too upset with the break-up, optimistically stating, "For now I'm on the single road again, which is a breath of fresh air."

Even the January 1994 wedding of her sister Dannii to actor Julian McMahon didn't appear to shake the singer, who happily took on the role of bridesmaid at the ceremony. "I was grinning like a Cheshire cat," she recalls. "I had sore cheeks I was so happy for them." During the wedding reception, the Minogue sisters performed a jubilant and rousing version of 'We Are Family' for the guests. Sadly Dannii and Julian's marriage would not last the year.

❤   ❤   ❤   ❤   ❤

Five years after her last film appearance, Kylie took on the role of British intelligence officer Cammy in the big screen adaptation of the popular arcade game, *Street Fighter*. She'd landed the role after director Steven de Sousa saw her picture on the cover of an Australian magazine listing *The 30 Most Beautiful People In The World*. Kylie shot her scenes in Queensland, where she became a fictional PA to Colonel Guile, played by Jean-Claude Van Damme. Together they lead an Allied Nations fighting force to victory.

To measure up to Van Damme's comic-book muscles and prepare her for the battle scenes, Kylie trained in martial-arts and weightlifting. She especially enjoyed blowing things up with a large bazooka gun, later recalling, "They bring in the guns and I'm like, Bam! Bam! Bam! The film crew are like, 'She didn't even *blink*. Even Mel Gibson blinks when he fires his gun...'" Unfortunately several scenes were cut, leaving her part as little more than eye-candy to momentarily detract from the banal plot.

As an American blockbuster, *Street Fighter* grossed some $70 million at the box office, but nobody noticed La Minogue in amongst the explosions and macho bravado. Nowadays Kylie refers to this film as her "Hollywood faux-pas."

> *"Basically I was put*
> *in tight clothes and*
> *I just stood there.*
> *I'm old enough – I should*
> *have known better."*

Cave had long since fostered an outspoken crush on the starlet

Sweeping this embarrassment under the proverbial carpet, Kylie drew on an old colleague to provide some much-needed credibility and famously slow danced with Prince to his hit, 'The Most Beautiful Girl In The World', at the post-World Music Awards party in Monte Carlo. Michael Hutchence and Helena Christensen looked on as Kylie proved to the world she too was a serious – and sexy – artist with good connections.

Again the press queried the true nature of Kylie's involvement with Prince, which was old news as far as she was concerned. Indeed over the summer of 1994 she fought off endless allegations of supposed romances. One source suggested she was about to marry John Lennon's son Julian, whom in truth she had met only once in an LA club. "He's a nice guy but no," she politely commented.

Next came the possible pairing of her with rubber-faced comedian, Jim Carrey. "I was at a restaurant in Los Angeles and someone at my table knew someone at his table," said Kylie. "He might have asked if I wanted to go over and sit at their table. I did. And that was that."

Then there was rock's wild man, Lenny Kravitz – again quite good for the old credibility. "There's a little bit of truth to that," confessed Kylie. "But we weren't going out together." After model Brent Waling, Kylie's final 'conquest' for the year came in the shape of Evan Dando, the lead singer from The Lemonheads. Like the stories about Kravitz, there was a little truth behind the myth. The two pop stars snogged at a club in Melbourne, and apparently disappeared into a toilet together for some time. Kylie later admitted to nothing more significant than simply "hanging out" with Dando for a couple of nights. "What can I say? There's actually not much to tell. I didn't have anything serious to do with him... but there was some frivolity." There would soon be little or no time for "frivolity" in Kylie's life.

September 1994 saw the release of Kylie's first single on the deConstruction label, 'Confide In Me'. Her fans had waited nearly two years for some new musical output from their star and they weren't disappointed. The swirling orchestral track, complete with its odd Japanese references and Kylie's brand new breathy singing style, shot straight to number two in the UK and number one in Australia, New Zealand, Finland, Croatia and Turkey. The colourful cartoon-meets-sex-phoneline video was in complete and baffling contrast to the song.

The comeback was swiftly followed by its parent album, simplistically entitled *Kylie Minogue*. "There were two options," Kylie explained when quizzed on the album's direction as a whole.

"❝**E**ither we could make another pop record or we could throw me into the field and just try anything. We chose the latter.❞"

Indeed, *Kylie Minogue* showcased the singer's best work so far, thanks to the influence of writers and producers including Brothers In Rhythm, Jimmy Harry, DJs Terry Farley and Pete Heller, M People and Pet Shop Boys. Kylie's name only appeared in one joint songwriting credit, for 'Automatic Love'. Having previously stated how important this part of her development was to her, now she meekly seemed to back down, explaining, "I enjoy writing but it's not something that I have to do when there are brilliant writers around. I would never choose a song that I had written above another song because I had done it. The best song wins."

Meanwhile Kylie's visual style had changed once more and the photos on the CD sleeve showed her crouching in a man's suit and oversized glasses, perhaps an attempt to appear more intellectual than beautiful – a deliberate step away from her previous PWL persona. The release of *Kylie Minogue* came in tandem with a Madonna-esque limited edition picture book showing Kylie in a variety of erotic poses. The book sold well. The album went to number four, moving a quarter of a million copies in the UK alone. The second single, 'Put Yourself In My Place', assisted by a *Barbarella*-style video, came in at a strong number 11. She was back.

After being crowned Most Desirable Human Being at *NME*'s BRAT awards in January 1995, along came an offer the newly-hip Kylie just could not afford to turn down.

Mushroom Records also handled the affairs of Michael Hutchence's old friend Nick Cave, the literate and much respected gothic indie rocker also from Australia. Cave had long since fostered an outspoken crush on the starlet and had wanted to work with her since she burst onto the Australian scene with 'The Loco-Motion'.

"I've always wanted to write Kylie a song, to have her sing something sad and slow," he mused. Up until now Kylie had resisted his attempts at a collaboration, saying, "I was always open to the idea but never actively pursued it. I figured it would just come around." But when Cave's demo of 'Where The Wild Roses Grow' arrived at Mushroom, she decided the time was ripe. The pair met at a studio in Melbourne and laid down the vocals for what was to become the duet of the year.

Far left: A newly-cropped Kylie in a promotional shot for 'Where The Wild Roses Grow' with Nick Cave
Above: Behaving frivolously with Lenny Kravitz

Kylie

Kylie with Nick Cave in 1995

"He's very charming," said Kylie of her new mentor. "It was an experience to work with him but, also, the way he made me perform was different to anything I've done.

"It's a really different vocal. You probably wouldn't know it was me at all."

"I'm really glad it happened." For Cave's part he later remarked, "I'd say that doing 'Wild Roses' with Kylie was the most important and enjoyable collaboration that I've done. I think she's quite remarkable. Working with her just seemed … right."

Two months later they met again in London, where Kylie contributed her delicate touch to Cave's forthcoming project, the *Murder Ballads* album, joining the ranks of Cave's other collaborators PJ Harvey and Shane MacGowan. Kylie's second track on the album after 'Where The Wild Roses Grow' was no lightweight affair: she participated in a cover of Bob Dylan's 'Death Is Not The End'.

Cave's influence on Kylie's acceptance into more grown-up rock circles cannot be underestimated, just like Michael Hutchence's sway years before. For a former dance queen to

successfully cross over to such a discerning audience was an extreme gamble, but the release of this new work could not come soon enough for Kylie. Although widely praised on home turf and in the UK for her latest album, in the States Imago had dropped *Kylie Minogue* from its major releases, seriously damaging any chance she had there of reinventing herself as an adult artiste.

While Kylie was in Australia recording with Nick Cave she met her next boyfriend, 35-year-old model and aspiring actor, Mark Gerber, who had recently appeared in *Sirens* alongside Hugh Grant and Elle Macpherson. His role was highly erotic with many of his scenes shot nude. Whether or not this was what attracted Kylie to him was anyone's guess, but soon enough the couple were seen out and about, and at gigs performed by Mark's band, Flame Boa.

Relations became a little strained when work obligations forced Kylie to leave Mark behind in Sydney. "It's a long-distance romance and at the moment my work is so much at the forefront of everything I do, any relationship is really secondary," she divulged to the press. "So it's not as it was, for no other reason than it's hard. Romance is wonderful and it's something I enjoy. I go on dates but I'm so content with my work, I couldn't be happier." She concluded by suggesting that this boyfriend wasn't necessarily for keeps. "I don't know if I prefer being single or in relationships but I'm having a ball right now."

Around this time reports – accompanied by some harrowing and damning pictures – surfaced in the press about Jason Donovan's drug-induced breakdown. After a year or two following in Kylie's SAW footsteps, Jason had carved out a brand new career in the West End, playing the lead in Andrew Lloyd Webber and Tim Rice's *Joseph And The Amazing Technicolor Dreamcoat* intermittently from 1991 to early 1994. But the excessive celebrity lifestyle had made a terrible impact on the former soap star and he collapsed at the Viper Room in LA while celebrating Kate Moss' birthday.

Kylie was concerned about her ex and commented in March 1995, "I think he's had a rough time. He's run into a bit of trouble. But maybe he likes trouble. The thing about Jason is, he's actually quite eccentric." Jason would collapse again that November near his home in Bondi Beach and had to be revived with oxygen by paramedics. Eventually, he cleaned up his act and became a devoted family man.

❤   ❤   ❤   ❤   ❤

> "*It's a good thing that acting is my profession, because I probably drive everybody mad. All day, every day, I'm possessed by various characters.*"

Undeterred by her experience in *Street Fighter*, as Kylie's schedule slowed, she again embraced acting. *Hayride To Hell* saw Kylie in her most unlikely role yet – as a raven-haired diabetic psychotic hitch-hiker who spends the 11 minutes of this extraordinary short film jumping on top of car bonnets, fainting and feigning violent attacks on a stranger with a teddy bear. Filming opposite Richard Roxburgh took just seven days in Sydney, and during that demanding week Kylie embodied the personality of her nameless character full time.

"Come the evening, there wasn't much time to switch off, so I was quite a beast for a while," she admitted. "My boyfriend was like, 'Who is this girl?' I think it's funny that I was pretty awful and I knew it, but I didn't want to let go of her too much. I guess

every actor goes through that but this was the first time I had it to that degree. Scared the life out of me – but I think I did a reasonable job."

Hayride To Hell was only screened at film festivals in London, Chicago and Telluride, but for Kylie it wasn't about the exposure, more the experience itself. "It's possibly one of the best experiences I've had in a while," she said. "I wanted the character to be believable and she was so different to anything that I've come across. Although there was obviously a part in me that thought, 'Great, I can expand on that.' Some madness somewhere."

As Kylie turned 27 in May 1995, another opportunity to reassert her skills as an actress arose. Her second Hollywood feature was to be *Bio Dome*, from the team who produced the hit gross-out movie, *Dumb And Dumber*. It tells the tale of two college simpletons played by Pauly Shore and Stephen Baldwin, who accidentally trap themselves for a year inside an environmentally controlled dome alongside five scientists. Kylie played Australian oceanographer Petra Von Kant, the butt of many a joke for the lead characters.

This was not Kylie's best career move. After all, she had fought long and hard to appear more intellectual through her music. Although during filming she gushed, "It's been so much fun, I swear I've just loved it," soon after it wrapped she began to voice her concerns. Primarily she disliked the fact that the loose storyline allowed for little plot or character progression, and that she had been unable to showcase her talents to her best ability.

"I've done two Hollywood films that have left me very disappointed and, seriously, I couldn't take another one," she complained. "They were fun, light-hearted, and I did them for American exposure, but these Hollywood things are like, 'Let's get her into something short and tight and do scenes that have very little relevance to each other.' I'm sure the right script will turn up but I'm not actively pursuing it."

It sounded almost as if the actress had given up her original profession entirely as a result of *Bio Dome*, which years later she professed not even to have properly seen. "You know how with parents, you can do something that's not so great, and they'll tell you they loved it?" she said. "My dad said, 'I can't believe you did that. That was just diabolical!' So I never watched it." Unsurprisingly *Bio Dome* flopped in the US that Christmas, and went straight to video in many other territories. Her bid for exposure didn't entirely fail as Kylie was consequently offered a part in the American soap *Central Park West*, but the girl had had enough, and politely turned it down.

Above: Kylie as Petra Von Kant in *Bio Dome*

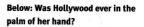

Below: Was Hollywood ever in the palm of her hand?

❤ • ❤ • ❤ • ❤ • ❤

Kylie's life was rarely without its ups and downs, and in mid-1995 her short-lived relationship with Mark Gerber dissolved. "I was always saying to him, 'You've got to do more acting,' bossy woman that I am," she later reflected. But the singing budgie was never destined to be alone for long, and in June she took off for a month's holiday, driving across America in a 1979 Trans-Am with a new friend, the French photographer Stephane Sednaoui. Although at that stage an affair was not strictly on the cards, rebound or not, Kylie fulfilled a romantic dream she had long harboured of following in her dad's footsteps. Ron Minogue had twice driven the same route in 1958 and 1961.

"I talk about doing a lot of things and never really do them, so this was one under my belt," said Kylie, later adding that her most treasured possession was a photo album given to her by Sednaoui cataloguing their adventure. "It was a journal of our trip across America."

> "*Driving a car across the States was one of my favourite experiences.*"

Far right: Bringing a new meaning to 'Sisters' with Elton John
Above right: Kylie shares a joke with Stephane Sednaoui
Below: With Nick Cave at T In The Park in Glasgow

For the rest of the summer Kylie maintained her profile by releasing a third single on deConstruction, the re-recorded 'Where Is The Feeling?', which reached number 16 in the UK (the song had previously been released in Japan, where it reached number four). In support of this and her forthcoming duet with Nick Cave, she performed alongside him at two music festivals; the Fleadh festival in Cork and the T In The Park festival in Glasgow. She was also seen duetting on the old Minogue favourite, 'Sisters Are Doin' It For Themselves' at a charity show at London's Royal Albert Hall, with Elton John in a beautiful blond wig as Dannii's replacement.

In October fans were delighted with the release of 'Where The Wild Roses Grow' – and a serious, sultry side to their beloved pop star was revealed. "I was more than happy to do it. It's a beautiful song," said Kylie of the haunting and sombre ballad, set unusually in 6/8 time. For the song and its accompanying video, Kylie is cast as Eliza Day, who speaks from beyond the grave to the lover who murdered her in cold blood. The video was quite risqué for the newly redheaded Kylie, who languished in a river wearing a virginal white slip, with both a snake and Cave's hands repeatedly caressing her body.

As far as image-altering went, it worked, and Kylie gained her much-coveted credibility within rock circles the world over. Although the song wasn't a chart-topper (number eleven in the UK and two in Australia), its lasting effect was certainly worth its weight in gold.

Elton John in a beautiful blond wig as Dannii's replacement

Kylie

CuteKylie

KYLIE'S BEEN AROUND FOR LONGER THAN you'd think: nearly 16 years. Like her self-acknowledged heroine, Madonna, she has experienced about as many changes in style as years she's been in the public eye. Normally it's a case of the media slapping a label on her forehead, and Kylie willingly goes along for the ride. She'll sell more records if she'll be the person her fans want her to be.

In 1997's video for 'Did It Again', the singer openly acknowledges CuteKylie, SexKylie, DanceKylie and IndieKylie: overblown, Barbie doll-like caricatures who fight for control over their maker. CampKylie prepared for battle a couple of years later.

"Style is your own interpretation of what you are and what you want to project to others. Often what you are isn't what you project."

SexKylie

DanceKylie

IndieKylie

style

RealKylie

CampKylie

CuteKylie

"My girlfriends say I'm like CuteKylie – she's like Miss Goody Goody.**"**

MAKE NO MISTAKE; THE EIGHTIES WERE an unforgiving fashion blunder. It was during this period that Kylie Minogue first made an impression on the world, and that's not something she's ever going to live down.

Reminiscing today, you have to feel sorry for her.

"The terrible photo shoots I used to do and the things I used to wear!**"**

"I feel at a great disadvantage," she wails. "Everybody knows what I looked like when I was a teen. I feel like shouting to the world, show me your photos at 17, show me what's hidden under your bed!"

Early SAW style packaged Kylie into a perfectly clean-cut girl-next-door. Cashing-in on her tomboyish portrayal of cheeky, fun-loving Charlene in *Neighbours*, not only must she continue to appeal to children and teenagers alike, but also both sexes. She should be pretty enough to catch the boys' eyes, but not so pretty that the girls rejected her. Most importantly she couldn't be too intimidating – sexiness or rebellion was not an option. So instead she was carefully moulded into something fluffy and lightweight – forget your mother, even your *grandmother* could approve if you liked Kylie Minogue.

Kylie's early videos showcased this non-threatening PR vision to a T. From late 1987 to early 1989, she screamed saccharine sweetness. Images of little Kylie forever imprinted on the public's conscious include: the bubble bath and graffiti spelling 'I Luv You' in 'I Should Be So Lucky'. The lime green miniskirt and kiss curl in 'Got To Be Certain'. The ra-ra skirt and big hair of 'The Loco-Motion'. The Shirley Temple period drama of 'Je Ne Sais Pas Pourquoi'. The cute country bumpkin of 'It's No Secret'. The matching heart-dress and stilettos – in red, yellow *and* blue – of 'Hand On Your Heart'.

"Like the *Top Of The Pops* performance where I had the biggest earrings on you've ever seen – like a bunch of grapes hanging from each ear. The era of puffball skirts – what a time to become famous!"

And what of the boyfriend she had to pretend was just a friend – Jason Donovan? Equally manufactured, with any hint of sex appeal painstakingly airbrushed out, there he was with his trendy ripped jeans and long golden hair. Filmed together for the duet 'Especially For You', they cuddle but don't kiss for the cameras. Interestingly, Kylie's face is virtually unrecognisable. Her features, although slim, do not yet display any definition of adulthood. Her eyebrows are bushy and shapeless, and her top lip traces a thin line over her large, yellowish teeth, giving her a rather goofy profile. All that would have to be fixed. She wears jeans and a T-shirt.

As with all of Kylie's images, no label (apart from, perhaps, IndieKylie) is assigned to a fixed date and the star enjoys revisiting old ground whenever the whim takes her. CuteKylie was last seen during the On A Night Like This Tour, where she milked her old songs for all they were worth. Picture a demure version of 'I Should Be So Lucky' where Kylie sits atop a baby grand piano, framed in a heart-shaped spotlight. She wears a white top hat and tails and gives us a glimpse of her former self; a little lost but not forgotten.

SexKylie

"SexKylie? She's filth, that one! She's horrible but she's fantastic. She's wrecked before the fight, if you know what I mean."

IT WAS ALL MICHAEL HUTCHENCE'S FAULT. He introduced Kylie to Sex, and CuteKylie was buried alongside Jason Donovan's pop career. "Sexiness is a part of me and I can play that character – putting it out, dripping in diamonds – and that's a lot of fun but it *is* a performance," Kylie reminds us. She is a *bona fide* actress, after all. "I find the camera a challenge and trying to be sexy in front of it when you're actually in a roomful of people gawping at you is hard work. But I like to challenge myself to do it well."

At the end of the Eighties, part of Kylie's challenge was to persuade SAW to allow her to deviate from girl-next-door. "Ever since finishing school, I'd done what I'd been told to do," she says. "I didn't have much of a say in my music. For a long time, changing my image was almost the only way I had to express myself." Like many students of her trade, she began by emulating others.

In the video for 'Wouldn't Change A Thing' Kylie becomes not one but two sex goddesses. Initially she vamps it up with a grown-up hairstyle and bright red lipstick, displaying for the first time a cleavage and draping a cross around her neck.

Far right: From the video for 'Step Back In Time' Above right and Below: Kylie favoured a Sixties style to make her sexier

"*Sexiness is a part of me and I can play that character*"

Right: From the single sleeve for
'What Do I Have To Do'
Far right: Kylie mixes her influences
and Sixties meets Madonna

62

When she changes to a white tasselled bra and beads it becomes clear she hopes to mimic Madonna. This footage is interspersed with a very different image, a wobbly home video in which she giggles and plays with a kitten in a garden. She may not resemble her physically, but the coquettish behaviour is very Marilyn Monroe.

This is where SexKylie's obsession with past screen queens began. Having worn a bouffant hairdo and archetypal Little Black Dress in the video for 'Tears On My Pillow', Kylie went full-on Sixties in the early Nineties. 'What Do I Have To Do?' sees her with black pencilled-in eyebrows, huge false eyelashes and a brand new pout. Collagen lip implants or clever makeup? We'll never know but she's suddenly a different person. When speaking of this look, Kylie admitted she aspired to being, "all-out glam ... as many movie stars as possible; Sophia Loren, Brigitte Bardot, Elizabeth Taylor..."

Marilyn Monroe returned for the short platinum curls in 'If You Were With Me Now', *And God Created Woman*'s Brigitte Bardot inspired the milkmaid creation of 'What Kind Of Fool', and as late as 1997 even Jane Fonda got a look-in as Kylie donned a hot pink spacesuit and *Barbarella*-style hair and makeup for 'Put Yourself In My Place'.

But it didn't all have to revolve around film stars. As soon as Kylie had found her size 3 feet, she was more than comfortable in the sex kitten role and it became the norm for videos like 'Shocked' and 'Word Is Out' to feature her being fondled by a faceless extra and dressed in nothing but lingerie and stilettos, sometimes even displaying a whiff of suspender belt or fishnet stocking. SexKylie lives on to this day with her recent on-tour performance of Olivia Newton-John's 'Physical', in which she is wheeled onstage on a four poster bed draped with female dancers wearing very little indeed. She proceeds to pole dance seductively around the bed posts – her very own version of soft porn. And why not embrace this side of her if it comes naturally?

" I don't try to be a sex bomb. I just am one. Sometimes. The rest of the time, I just like loafing around."

SexKylie

When she changes to a
white tasselled bra and beads
it becomes clear she hopes
to mimic Madonna

DanceKylie

Another persona was adopted to appeal to her vigorously fit club audience

> "*All the styles I've experimented with were just me trying to work out who I was. In the early days, my image was the only part of my career I could get my mitts on, which is why it took such a tumultuous turn.*"

WHEN SHE WASN'T BEING SEXKYLIE, another persona was adopted to appeal to her vigorously fit club audience. DanceKylie was born with the Hi-NRG beats of 'Better The Devil You Know'. Alongside her scanty costumes, Kylie could now experiment with wigs and street fashions in amongst the strobe lights and not compromise her sex appeal.

In fact the Seventies-themed attire of Kylie and her dancers in 1990's 'Step Back In Time' video inspired style bible *Vogue* to devote an entire six-page spread to her in their Christmas issue that year. Having previously accused the slender pop star of being anorexic, it was now politically correct for such magazines to quiz her on her fitness and diet secrets, so that readers could try them out for themselves. They wouldn't like the answers. "I don't go to the gym and I don't do anything to keep myself in trim," Kylie might blithely declare. "It's just my general non-stop lifestyle." Sometimes quoted as enjoying anything from kick boxing and roller-skating to snowboarding and in-line skating, the truth remains more of the couch potato kind. "I don't work out but touring keeps me fit," she said at the end of 2001. "That's next year. At the moment if I go up a flight of stairs I'm gasping."

As for the diet, forget it. "I eat junk food, pretty much anything I want – dark chocolate, chips, ice cream," boasts the 7st 2lbs Aussie who literally can't get fat. "I need to keep my weight up or else I go too skinny, and trust me, that doesn't look good at all."

Above, left and far left: Madonna was clearly a big influence for Kylie's rigorous dance routines

IndieKylie

Indie Kylie

> "At several points in my career I have tried to create images that just weren't right, that just weren't me. But my fans say, 'Oh, it's just Kylie going through one of her phases. Don't worry, she'll get over it.' They seem to appreciate that I tried something and it didn't work. But at least I tried!"

KYLIE IS THE FIRST PERSON TO recognize that her style changes with the man she's dating. If Jason Donovan helped flavour CuteKylie and Michael Hutchence flagrantly inspired SexKylie, then cutting-edge photographer Stephane Sednaoui may well have provided the basis for IndieKylie.

Says our subject, "Well, they *were* the three main loves of my life and the three stages when I did the most changing. I'm not ashamed to admit that when I'm with a boyfriend I take on board some of their personality. And Stephane, being creative, introduced me to the visual world of fashion."

IndieKylie was sadly short lived. It involved chopping off her long blonde hair and experimenting with short, boldly coloured styles during her years at deConstruction. An early glimpse of Kylie's forthcoming incarnation came in the video for 'Confide In Me', in which she sported a frizzy blonde afro and heavy comic-strip makeup – a new, colourful personality for the masses.

Retreating for a while behind the smudged kohl eyes of 'Where Is The Feeling', a blatant copy of Madonna's 'Cherish' (both singers get wet on a beach in black and white), IndieKylie soon returned with all of the artwork for her second deConstruction album, *Kylie Minogue*. In the video for 'Some Kind Of Bliss' she had cropped red hair, and didn't seem to care too much about her appearance, driving across the desert in her dusty denims. On the album cover she was – shock – a mousy haired medusa with spikes and swirls.

Although Kylie was willing to try, it soon became apparent that her audience didn't appreciate this particular attempt at cool. Just before she parted company with deConstruction for good, Kylie discovered camp while onstage in Sydney: "What the audience responded to was the pop when

I had pink feathers on my head, being a showgirl. It wasn't when I had choppy, dark hair and wore loads of eyeliner. Because of the way everything had turned out, I thought, 'I have to be myself.' And if that's going to appear uncool, 'daggy' or high camp, then so be it. I still have to do it."

**Below: On her way to meet George Michael for dinner at The Ivy restaurant in London
Right: Kylie attends the Ivor Novello Awards**

IndieKylie was sadly short lived

IndieKylie

IndieKylie involved experimenting with make-up, hair colour and style
Far right: Kylie poses in front of a promotional poster for *Kylie Minogue* II

CampKylie

"I do think I am the girl on the show pony sometimes. A best friend described me as the girl at the circus on the pony, striking a pose."

The 'On A Night Like This' tour visits the Hammersmith Apollo

THE EARLIEST-KNOWN VERSION OF CampKylie can be seen in her 1989 video for 'Never Too Late'. At that time completely unaware of the large pocket of gay fans she was attracting and the transvestite 'Kylie Nights' in her home country, the starlet was really only playing with a dressing-up box as, backed by two butch dancers, she tried her hand at being a Twenties-style flapper, a cowgirl, a Chinese lady and a hippy. It was straight out of Village People's 'YMCA'.

A decade later came the disco reinvention of *Light Years* and CampKylie returned. This time her image was fully intentional. "The album was about re-establishing and reminding myself of what I do and generally indulging in the shininess, pinkness and campness of that side of my personality and of pop," she beamed. "And I loved it."

So out came the hot pants, accompanied by Farrah Fawcett flicks and gold sparkles for the notorious 'Spinning Around' video. Suddenly she was just fabulous, dahling, and neither heterosexual nor homosexual men could resist those shimmying buttocks. But there was a surprise in store – girls liked it too.

"When 'Spinning Around' came out, I was so surprised," she says. "So many girls and women came up to me and said, 'We love your song, you look so great and so sexy in that video.' And it really touched me that they weren't saying, 'Huh, what's she doing strutting around in those shorts making all of us feel insecure?' They weren't like that at all. I was their mate."

In the words of her erstwhile producer Pete Waterman, "If it ain't broke, don't fix it." Kylie embraced Camp, or was it the other way round? Her On A Night Like This Tour saw her female dancers dressed in bikinis and grass hula skirts, which were later removed. They were the lucky ones – the boys

(all notably under 5'6") modelled a dazzling array of Jean-Paul Gaultier-style sailor suits, black string vests and American football shoulder pads. The best costumes came out during the gay anthem, 'Your Disco Needs You', in which they marched on dressed as rugby players wearing flags for skirts... which were later removed.

Kylie flourished amidst the kitsch – being lowered from the ceiling on a large blue anchor to start the show, and ravishing in her own array of sequins, satin kimonos, bikinis and some dashing red leather flares. In the accompanying video, *Live In Sydney*, she even credited herself as 'Showgirl'.

Suddenly
she was just fabulous, dahling

*There's not a wrinkle
or spare inch of flesh on her*

> "*I enjoy putting on the gear and playing the star — to me it's all dress-ups. But as soon as I get home I wipe my face off, get my track pants on, and I'm no longer Kylie The Product; I'm a real person again.*"

NOT QUITE READY TO LEAVE LABELS behind, most recently Kylie enthrals her public with an eye-catching white hooded number slashed to the waist in the video for 'Can't Get You Out Of My Head'. It's a heady mix of CampKylie and SexKylie, and fans should expect more of the same for the upcoming 'In Your Eyes' video, which is all about flashing disco lights and Kylie wearing... not very much.

Diet and fitness aside, there's not a wrinkle or spare inch of flesh on her, which isn't bad for a 33-year-old with such a hectic lifestyle. "It's all done with mirrors," she laughs. "When I'm making a video, I want to look as good as I can so I make friends with the lighting guys!" Surely even hi-tech equipment can't design what isn't there in the first place. Has she never heard of cellulite? "Let's just say I'm a woman and part of being a woman is having to battle with that. And it's the kind of battle we tend to lose."

Once upon a time, a younger version of today's siren claimed she would begin to "cover up" when she hit the ripe old age of 30. If anything, she now wears 100 per cent less clothing, so what prompted the change of heart? "I was probably preparing for the worst, thinking that everything would have gone south by then," she explains. "But as it turned out, I didn't have to. I'm so small that if I've got a lot of clothes on I'm not that comfortable." Kylie's sickening self-assurance, she reveals, comes from getting older and she's not afraid to face her future.

> "*Ageing doesn't bother me. Age is about being confident with who you are.*"

Over the last few years, Kylie has posed in any number of scantily-clad pictures for worshipping lads' mags – "I always end up in my knickers in a photo shoot!" – and her image gets raunchier by the minute. Kylie's version of events is that she's not that much of a turn-on anyway. "I think I get away with that because people have known me for so long, I'm like safe sex," she says. "There's nothing that domineering about me.

"I think you could put someone else in the same outfit and the same pose and it would be read a completely different way. It's like I'm winking, and I'm not winking." She graciously admits to a few

Far left: The Real Kylie shows her face
Below: Kylie poses with her updated Madame Tussaud's waxwork

"I always end up in my knickers in a photo shoot!"

Kylie

Far right: Wowing the audience at the *Smash Hits* Poll Winners Party, London Arena
Right: Kylie attends the *Moulin Rouge!* premiere
Below: Casual chic

imperfections, "I wish I was blessed with Latin-type, big, strong, beautiful hair, but I have my mother's hair," and "I have my own insecurities about my body, of course I do – but I'm mostly fine with it. It's the Australian in me; the lifestyle's more open about showing our bodies."

Now an undisputed queen of style, Kylie can pick and choose from the world's leading designers. Close friend Julien Macdonald fashioned the silver half-dress she wore at the European MTV Music Awards. Australian designer Collette Dinnigan created the stylish black and beige dress she wore to the premiere of *Moulin Rouge!* and she also favours Chloe, Ungaro and Versace.

For her footwear, Kylie is equally particular, and parades in Manolo, Jimmy Choo, Patrick Cox, Dolce & Gabbana, Prada and Gucci shoes. After all, there are websites out there devoted entirely to her feet, set up after she commented, "I've had girlfriends curse me about my feet. They're not normally the prettiest things, but mine aren't bad at all."

Style icon or not, the thing with Kylie is that we have all witnessed her trials and tribulations of growing up, and her progression through label after label. She could never be accused of not trying something different, and most of the time she comes out smiling.

As she honestly sums up herself,

"*Although I can assume the glamorous and sexy role, there's still a part of me which allows people to approach me in the street and go, 'Alright Kyles, how are you?'*"

Chapter 8: No World Without You

"The important thing is choice.
You might decide you'd like some help, but that's your decision."

T THE BEGINNING OF 1996 KYLIE TURNED her attention to her next album on deConstruction. With her collaborative success with Nick Cave fresh in her mind she now endeavoured to record with the hippest, trendiest musicians she could find.

"My daytime fantasy is to have an album where I can work with the likes of Blur and Nick Cave and some American artists, like 10 different bands of all different styles, and just see what they would do with me," she pondered. "It would be like giving 10 sculptors a piece of rock. It would mean a bit of a regression for me, because that [manipulation] is exactly what I was trying to escape. But as an experimental thing, it would be very interesting."

Equally, after many years of being persuaded otherwise, it was time to write her own material.

First came James Dean Bradfield and Sean Moore from Manic Street Preachers. Together they wrote tracks called 'Some Kind Of Bliss' and 'I Don't Need Anyone'. Manic Street Preachers had wanted to work with Kylie for years, having asked her to sing on their song, 'Little Baby Nothing'. Unfortunately their faxed request never reached her as it had been sent via SAW, and instead ex-porn star Traci Lords sent that song to number 29 in 1992.

Finally together, Kylie became good friends with Bradfield who, in a similar vein to Nick Cave, adopted her as his muse. She was becoming a trend by association. "They're attracted by... whatever," said Kylie, grateful if a little baffled. "I find that I don't even want to try and invent rationales for why they came to me, it's just magical enough that they did. Perhaps I was good in a past life. Or, more likely, I'm just a very, very lucky person." The Cave connection also continued, with him writing a track to which she added lyrics, but for some reason it would not be released.

Kylie again worked with Brothers In Rhythm,

now joining them as a co-writer with equal billing. Much of her material was dark and self-questioning, but a look at her private life reveals its source.

In between love affairs, Kylie had begun to query the meaning of her chaotic life. On one hand she rejected her past associations with SAW and *Neighbours*, still referred to in each and every interview, yet on the other she could tell her relationship with deConstruction was not quite as rosy as she had once hoped. Unsure of her true direction, which she felt was vaguely indie, Kylie was suppressing a lot of strong, often negative feelings which she needed to get out of her system.

"That album was difficult," she later reflected. "It wasn't a happy time in my life. I felt I was alone. I didn't have the help I needed." Rattling off the lyrics to songs like 'Too Far' and 'Limbo' at breakneck speed, Kylie's own words are painfully telling, screaming out for help.

"Definitely on some songs,
lyrically it's obvious to me now
that I am saying,
'I'm not waving. I am, in fact, drowning.
Hello? Is anybody there?'"

"At the time I felt like there was no one to help me. I didn't have the support of the record company. Nothing gelled on that record."

The album, which was to be titled *Impossible Princess*, took nearly two years to make, leaving Kylie apprehensive about the fate of her career. "It will be odd to hear my own hopes and fears on the radio. I'm never sure how much I should say."

When Kylie was not toiling over *Impossible Princess*, the rest of 1996 was a pivotal year for two reasons. The first was the beginning of an intense affair with Stephane Sednaoui. The second was that in July Kylie experienced what she would later describe as her "moment of catharsis".

Following the release of *Murder Ballads* in February, Nick Cave had kept in touch with Kylie. "I'd somehow developed this relationship with Nick whereby he would sometimes call me up and say, 'I've just written this song and I'd like you to sing the chorus, OK? I'll see you tomorrow!'" she recalls. "So it was no real surprise to get a call from him in 1996 when he was doing a recital at the Poetry Olympics at the Royal Albert Hall." To Kylie's horror, Cave, a published poet in his own right, suggested she should recite the lyrics to 'I Should Be So Lucky'.

"I told him I'd think about it, that maybe we could just play it by ear and see what happened.

through some embarrassing moments together, but you know what? You're OK.' It was a real relief. I came to embrace and be proud of the past and the history that I'd been trying so hard to run away from, and stopped trying to be someone different."

Having lived for so long in England, Kylie finally seemed to have developed that element so intrinsic to the British sense of humour: irony. And it suited her.

Stephane Sednaoui had been part of Kylie's social circle for a while. The tall Frenchman appealed to the artistic side of the singer. "Stephane, being a photographer and very visual, introduced me to the fashion world and helped me become more sure of myself," she said.

After being spotted together at various functions throughout the year, in December 1996 Kylie admitted to the press:

Far left and below: Kylie finally admitted to being in love with Stephane Sednaoui

> "Yes I'm in love. Stephane is wonderful, adorable and inspirational. I need kindness, spontaneity and sincerity in a man and I've got all three in Stephane. Plus he's successful and driven too. I admire that."

But the whole time I was thinking, 'I am not going to step out in front of London's literary world at the Albert Hall; they won't know who I am and it's just not going to work.'" But Mr Cave proved extremely persuasive, challenging the singer to face her demons – her past personas from *Neighbours* and SAW. Despite herself, Kylie turned up on the day.

"I remember I had to go on after a bearded blind man who was reciting his work from Braille," she continues. "I turned to Nick backstage and said, 'Nick, God is on stage! How am I supposed to follow that?', and he said, 'Well, Jesus did an OK job!' So I went on stage...

"I was in my tracksuit pants without a scrap of make-up on and a sticker with my name written on it. I was stripped of the usual preparations and securities of a performer, without the normal ego jacket that lets you go out and be the person you think your fans want you to be."

As Kylie deadpanned the rather basic lyrics to the song which had made her famous so many years before, she realised that she needn't have worried. "The crowd response was amazing; they laughed with me, not at me, and that night I learned to accept who I am. It was like meeting the old me face-to-face and saying, 'Alright, yes, we've been

Stephane was also the only person to address Kylie by her proper name – all her other friends always call her 'Min'.

Fortunately the language barrier wasn't a problem. "We would hardly ever speak French together, but when I did he would crumble," laughs Kylie. "He'd say, 'Oh, that sounds so *cute*,' because when you speak French as an Australian, you have an accent like a French person does when they are speaking English." Nevertheless, Kylie would include in the liner notes to *Impossible Princess* the message: "Stephane, merci et je t'adore."

Not for the first time reporters suggested the Australian superstar was preparing to marry, but Kylie, now 28, always denied such excitable claims with refreshing candour. "For me, I don't think there is such a thing as a perfect soulmate forever," she said. "Stephane is perfect for me at this time, but perhaps in a few years he might not be and that would be OK. I really believe that people go along

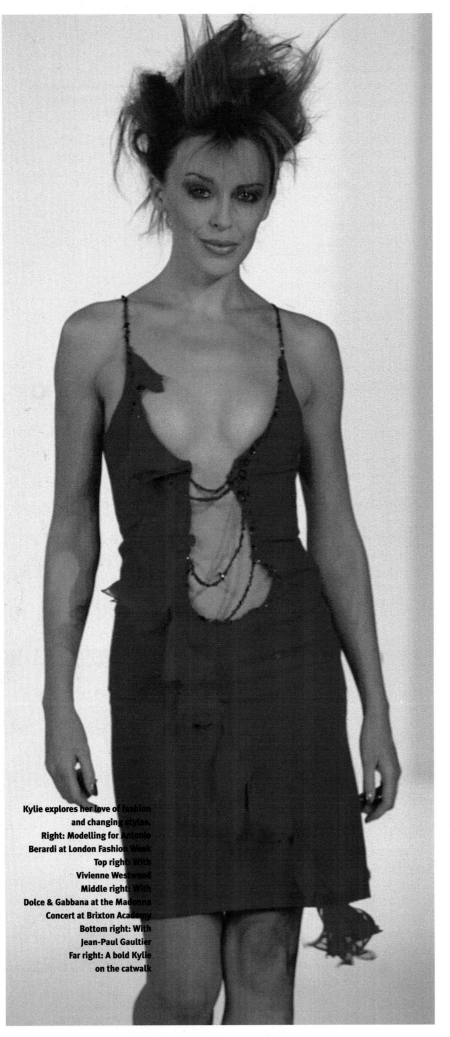

Kylie explores her love of fashion
and changing styles.
Right: Modelling for Antonio
Berardi at London Fashion Week
Top right: With
Vivienne Westwood
Middle right: With
Dolce & Gabbana at the Madonna
Concert at Brixton Academy
Bottom right: With
Jean-Paul Gaultier
Far right: A bold Kylie
on the catwalk

«Stephanie, being a photographer and more visual, introduced me to the fashion world»

parallel paths for a while and then one might veer off and run parallel with somebody else. I don't know why I think like this. Mum and Dad have been together for years and are still very much in love."

Impossible Princess was set for release in September 1997, and before that Kylie was involved in only one other project; a short film directed by the British artist, Sam Taylor-Wood. *Misfit* was far removed from anything Kylie had done before as it involved her miming naked to a recording made in Latin by the last castrato. It seemed everything the singer touched turned to gold, and the BBC enthusiastically described her performance as full of "erotic power and sexual ambiguity." Taylor-Wood

Below: Kylie attends Michael Hutchence's funeral on November 27, 1997 at St Andrew's Cathedral, Sydney

later wrote to Kylie praising her as, "a multi-faceted chameleon with the ability to hold the attention of anyone from my daughter to the *Evening Standard*-seller on the corner... you were the only person I could use for my piece."

All Kylie's plans ground to a halt on August 31, 1997 with the untimely death of Princess Diana in a chilling car crash. The world exploded with grief and it would have been highly inappropriate to release *Impossible Princess*, especially with such a newly-gauche title. For Kylie's team this was particularly bad news as the decision scuppered a promotional campaign that was already in full swing, demanding reprints of all the albums and related artwork and postponing the launch. "I could be upset about it, but then you have to look at the bigger picture and I have no right to be annoyed," said Kylie. "It's been delayed because a tragedy occurred. It was a reality check."

It was too late, however, to stop it all. 'Some Kind Of Bliss', Kylie's collaboration with Manic Street Preachers and the first single to be lifted from her now unnamed album entered the UK charts at number 22. The song, vastly different in sound and appeal from any previous Kylie track, was accompanied by an extreme change in image with a short auburn crop hairstyle and a *Thelma And Louise*-style video in which our heroine drives across the desert.

But the British public was in no mood to spend money on frivolities after Diana's death, and 'Some Kind Of Bliss' sank without trace soon after it first appeared. Kylie remained positive. "Though I have no illusion that I'm anything other than pop, I'm so much from that world that I don't think I'd ever be perceived as actually non-commercial," she stressed. "But any kind of progress requires sacrifice of some nature. A number one single again would be fantastic. But driving myself crazy in a bid to replicate my past successes would be pointless."

Instead she turned her attention to a fresh project which had no attachment to her seemingly doomed album. After some playful e-mail correspondence with Deee-lite DJ Towa Tei, Kylie recorded a wacky club track called 'GBI' with him. The initials stood for 'German Bold Italic', a computer font, and contained samples from Deee-lite's hit, 'Groove Is In The Heart'. Kylie filmed a promo video to go with the song, in which she was dressed bizarrely as an albino geisha girl under Stephane Sednaoui's direction. Originally released in Japan in September, where it became very successful, the oddity was later rereleased in the UK in October 1998 credited to Towa Tei Featuring Kylie Minogue and peaking at number 63.

In November 1997 Kylie took a trip back home

to Australia, where she found herself fending off unwanted attention resulting from an unauthorised biography by Sydney rock journalist Dino Scatena. It was, said Kylie, "so wrong. I never read it, but I've had parts of it relayed to me and, as diabolical as my memory is, I *do* remember how I lost my virginity – and it wasn't how it happened in that book!"

But if Kylie thought the events of the last couple of months were bad, there was worse to come. On November 22, 1997 the music world reeled with the startling news that Michael Hutchence had committed suicide in his suite at the Ritz-Carlton hotel in Sydney. He was 37.

The shocking manner of Michael's death opened a can of worms that was to torment his last partner, Paula Yates (Bob Geldof's ex-wife and mother of Michael's only child Heavenly Hiraani Tiger Lily), until her own death three years later. After a harrowing day in which Hutchence had engaged in heated debate regarding the custody of Yates' and Geldof's three children, drunk vodka, beer and champagne and taken cocaine and Prozac, he hung himself from a door using his belt. The buckle broke causing death by asphyxiation and his naked corpse was found kneeling on the floor by a maid. Due to Hutchence's consumption of drugs and alcohol and his well-known sexual appetite, an unpleasant by-product of his suicide was that for a while the press bandied about unfounded suggestions that Hutchence had been attempting a dangerous experiment involving auto-eroticism.

Kylie was devastated. Pale and utterly distraught she attended his funeral at St Andrew's Cathedral in Sydney, on November 27th. There she joined Hutchence's other loves and members of the rock aristocracy, including Paula Yates, Helena Christensen, members of INXS and Midnight Oil, Bono, Tom Jones and Nick Cave. The latter, an erstwhile business partner of Hutchence and Tiger Lily's godfather, sang a moving rendition of 'Into My Arms'.

"I learnt so much from Michael, and even now he's teaching me something new," said Kylie tearfully after the event.

"Michael's still around, I know that. People might think I'm mad, but I feel his presence. It's very personal. I feel him watching over me very strongly sometimes. He checks in with me and it's typical of him that I feel his presence when I need him most or just when something appropriate happens. It's not spooky, it's reassuring – although the force of his presence can be scary."

In 2002 Kylie revealed that it was this very presence that got her through the dark hours of the funeral service. "I haven't sensed him for a little while, but I do, and I did on the morning of his funeral. I've never gone into it in detail because it's too personal, but I had a real amazing experience: a feeling and a reaction in my body, and what I felt he was saying was, 'It's OK.' "

> "*It wasn't goodbye. It was comforting. I feel really lucky and thankful when he comes by.*"

❤   ❤   ❤   ❤   ❤

Life had to continue and in December 1997 the single 'Did It Again' was released, Kylie's cheerfulness in its promotion belying her inner suffering. Following on from her cathartic experience at the Poetry Olympics, Kylie stated that both song

> "*He's teaching me how to let go of someone I loved.*"

Although the couple had broken up years before, they had remained close friends and in Kylie's mind he had been the single greatest influence in her life. Then, a while after the funeral she began to speak about an unnerving after-effect of her former love's departure.

and video, which featured four Kylie incarnations (CuteKylie, SexKylie, IndieKylie and DanceKylie) engaging in battle, was about "not learning from your mistakes. In the video I'm telling myself off for making the same mistakes through my career, with my different images. What you see now is the real

"I don't create a scene, I just go quiet. And as my girlfriend pointed out, that makes just as much noise as yelling and screaming."

Kylie – I think!" So which Kylie was closest to the truth? "Well, my girlfriends say I'm like CuteKylie – she's like Miss Goody Goody, then something goes wrong and she turns nasty but ends up crying by the end," the singer revealed. Thanks to some excellent remixes, the singled fared better than 'Some Kind Of Bliss' and reached number 14 in the UK.

Kylie's *annus horribilis* had one more heartbreaking hand left to deal. As 1997 drew to a close, so did her two-year relationship with Stephane Sednaoui. The mutual split occurred because, in her words, he wasn't "what she'd hoped for."

As she had proved with Michael and Jason beforehand, Kylie wasn't the type to exclude a past love from her life, and the two remained friends.

"It's not easy to find someone that profound,"

she said years later. "We still have a great love for each other. We're in contact and depend on each other in lots of ways."

One interesting result of the split with Stephane was that Kylie literally coloured in her life. Previously her Chelsea home had been styled in minimalist white, but now she set about painting its front awning 'Lipstick' red, the front room pistachio and the kitchen in pale pink. Her furniture did not escape the vibrant treatment either and the kitchen bench, for example, became a deep chocolate colour. "My house had been white forever," she said. "When I broke up with Stephane, I wanted colour. I broke through!"

Although the split was harmonious, the end of this most difficult period in her life sparked an unsurprising collapse. "The last big cry I had was on New Year's Eve," she recalled. "I didn't have a very good year. I'd not had much that was sad in my life, but with Michael at the end of last year, and just

being exhausted with work, come New Year's Eve, I let it all out."

She continued with a revealing insight into her psyche, "I can be very changeable. Everything's fine, everything's fine, nothing's fine. That will last for a short while, and then I'll be as perky as can be again. Ninety-nine per cent of the time I'm a very happy person, then when I'm not, I don't create a scene, I just go quiet. And as my girlfriend pointed out, that makes just as much noise as yelling and screaming."

**Right: At the BRIT Awards, 1997
Far right: Opening a new branch
of Tower Records in Camden**

88

Chapter 9: Limbo

"Now I just know when something isn't right for me and when something is and what goals I still want to aim for"

Below: Kylie toasting her gay husband, William Baker
Far right: Having fun with Tim Jeffries

WHEN KYLIE WAS FEELING LOW, there were two people to whom she knew she could always turn; her parents. So that's exactly what she did at the beginning of 1998 with the horrors of 1997 still fresh in her mind.

"They're my two favourite fans, along with Dannii and my brother," she said recently. "They're not pushy showbiz parents, they're mum and dad and have always been there for me. A few years ago, when I was really stressed out and really needed them, I called them and said, 'Don't panic, it's OK, but I just wondered if you could come to London for two weeks. I'd really like to see you.' So even though Dad hates flying, they came over and I felt better. The best advice he ever gave me was that I could just say, 'No.' Now I just know when something isn't right for me and when something is and what goals I still want to aim for."

definitely no strings attached. "I've got a gay husband," she would say with a giggle. "Every girl should have one – gay is the new black."

So it was in this re-energized frame of mind that Kylie oversaw the long-awaited release of *Impossible Princess* in March, re-titled confusingly (and rather naffly), *Kylie Minogue* – the same as her last album. Despite the delay, it entered the UK charts at number 10 accompanied by the single 'Breathe' at number 14. After an initially good start, the album proceeded to baffle critics and fans alike and sold poorly. The general verdict was the music was too dark, too cluttered and too personal, and failed to charm in the legendary Minogue manner.

Kylie was deeply disappointed, but defended her baby to the hilt. "It wasn't the happiest period of my life," she said. "I was lost. It was messy. The record company went bust and I didn't get the help I needed," she continued, indicating the upcoming parting of ways with deConstruction.

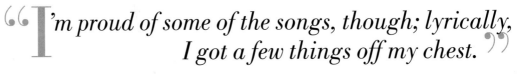

"I'm proud of some of the songs, though; lyrically, I got a few things off my chest."

Rejuvenated by the touch of home, Kylie began her New Year as she intended to go on: smiling. Straight out of a long-term relationship, the pop icon was soon seen strutting her stuff on the arms of a string of eligible bachelors. The first was no less than the Green Shield Stamps millionaire, Tim Jeffries, often humorously described as a "serial supermodeliser". He was followed in quick succession by *Muriel's Wedding* star Daniel Lapaine and various other macho accessories.

But this was all just fun and games for Kylie, who felt she deserved some light relief. In truth, the man she was turning to nowadays was her best friend and stylist, William Baker, and there were

Looking back on this experimentation after the passage of time, she remains satisfied that at least she'd tried. "It might be an album that in years some people will listen to a bit more and read into it things even I have overlooked or failed to tell them. I think there's definitely some good parts on the album, I just don't think it was cohesive at all. At least it's an indication of that time in my life. It isn't pretending.

"I was trying all different styles to see which suited me when I should have been sticking to what I knew best – doing pop songs. That's a lot clearer to me now I've got some distance from it. I don't regret anything though and I shouldn't be hard on myself, because before that, my track record is gleaming!"

*Kylie began her New Year
as she intended to go on: smiling*

Kylie

Right and far right: Kylie camping it up with some fellow showgirls

Always one to see a silver lining, Kylie's eventual admission that she should return to her pop roots was perhaps underlined by the release this year of *50+1*, possibly the worst Kylie compilation ever issued and proof to the resigned singer that she just could not shake her past.

"The Japanese made this hits CD called *50+1* which had snippets of 51 of my songs all done in a very Japanese way where they would speed up one song and then slow down the next. They had scraped together everything and half the songs that were on there I have no recollection of doing. It's so terrible that it has a certain charm – it's like an endurance test down memory lane!"

♥　♥　♥　♥　♥

"I love being a kitsch icon. I'm so camp sometimes – I feel I've missed my calling. Put me in an Esther Williams water routine – I'd love it! I'd have loved to be Judy Garland."

Despite the apparent failure of *Kylie Minogue II*, Kylie still had legions of devoted fans and she wasn't about to disappoint them. As she prepared for a promotional tour, her spirit was kept alive by constant references in the hit BBC comedy, *Men Behaving Badly*, starring Neil Morrissey and Martin Clunes as lads obsessed with all things Kylie. The singer was flattered and agreed to appear in a special charity edition, playing herself in an episode in which she visits the boys' flat, but they fail to

recognise her until after she's left. Previously she'd appeared in an episode of the Dawn French TV comedy *The Vicar Of Dibley*, turning up at the last minute to sing at the village fête.

Kylie's 1999 tour (later named *Intimate And Live* for the accompanying video and CD) showcased yet another new direction for Kylie – but this one she would keep. Consulting with William Baker, Kylie decided to go all-out camp.

"I remember William and I knocked off these sketches of what the stage should be like, the costumes, and we thought, why not go for it? William said, 'Just be yourself. Do the stairs – and the stairs must light up – do the feathers, do an hour-and-a-half show in stilettos every night.' OK, that might be looked on as totally uncool, but why shouldn't I be all those things? And I realised that I can move forwards only when I accept my past. It was a really important tour for me." So out came the sequins, the posturing and the revealingly garish costumes, and Kylie was A Star Reborn.

It was only fitting that in the midst of all this excitement, Kylie should celebrate her 30th birthday, greeting it with a warm handshake. "I loved turning 30," she recalls. "I was just about to start my tour in Australia and I felt good. I felt confident. I felt inspired. I felt like I knew myself more than before." The tour proved her most successful to date.

Drawing on her biggest hits and most embarrassing looks of the past, Kylie updated the likes of 'I Should Be So Lucky', 'Shocked' and 'The Loco-Motion' and witnessed the wild appreciation of her Australian audiences that May.

"It was the first time in a long time that I'd been in a room with not only an audience, but with people who've followed what I've been doing for years – people I'd grown up with, in a way," she recalls. "And what they responded to was the pop when I had pink feathers on my head, being a showgirl."

The background of Kylie's tour was slightly marred because she was without a UK record contract. Following the release of 'Cowboy Style' from *Kylie Minogue* II in Australia only, it was announced that she would no longer be working for deConstruction, which was, in her own words, "deconstructing". If it weren't for her amazing success on tour, the future might have looked bleak for the 30-year-old artist, who in the early days with SAW had sold over two million copies of her debut album, but had managed only 60,000 of her latest offering.

Above: With Rupert Penry-Jones, whom she met in Barbados performing *The Tempest*

"You become like family with a record company," she says today, "but I wanted to move. Looking back, it's all really clear. Every time I went into the office, someone I knew had left and there was someone else new I hadn't met. I felt quite... alone a lot of the time. The whole thing was a slight debacle." Still, as was her way, the separation was amicable.

"I parted with deConstruction after a long, and mainly happy, time together because we didn't achieve what we wanted to achieve with the last album. There are no fingers being pointed; I made mistakes, they made mistakes. It was a harmonious split for both parties and at no point did I consider it to be the end of my musical career. Besides, I wasn't without a deal for long..."

While she shopped around for a new label, Kylie immersed herself in projects for which she hadn't previously had time. Towards the end of 1998 she became involved in a children's charity, registering the name Kid Link with her father and planning to launch a telephone helpline for kids in crisis. Then she found out a similar organisation had already started, so decided to join in their crusade as an ambassador for the cause.

"It's a great charity," she said of Kids Help Line which averages around 35,000 calls a week and is manned by counsellors trained in issues such as suicide, drug and physical abuse, grief, violence and divorce. "I believe when you're successful, you've got to give something back. I often wondered if I could have any effect, but the fact is that celebrity has power, and it's a way to help. Some people help out at a fête or do volunteer work or throw money in the busker's hat. I know I can be of value with my name and presence. For me, if one person makes a call to the helpline and is helped, even in a small way, then it's wonderful, priceless."

While Kylie was happy to donate precious time to charity, she still needed to keep the bucks rolling in, and signed a contract with H&M Hennes to advertise their Christmas lingerie collection. The lads from *Men Behaving Badly* would have been proud. But aside from the posters of surely the tiniest ever fashion model baring her undies (and launching what would become an ongoing trend for La Minogue) little was seen or heard of Kylie for nearly a year to come.

Quietly in the background, Kylie reassessed her career. Although dropped from deConstruction in the UK, she was still signed to the Australian branch of Mushroom records, and in early 1999 negotiations commenced to begin working with them on a global scale. However, by April it was announced she had instead signed to Parlophone, a division of the giant label EMI, and was continuing with Mushroom in Australia. The decision came as a surprise to many, as Parlophone was home to bands like Radiohead, Supergrass and Blur, and Kylie was their first ever 'pop' signing – for that was what she had decided to do next. One thing that helped clinch the deal was Kylie's newfound self-confidence, well-honed after a year of poking fun at herself and appreciating what she stood for.

"This wasn't the MD of Parlophone," said Kylie of the meeting that sealed her fate. "It was the head of EMI! The real bigwig. The biggest wig. He said, 'The thing is Kylie, we don't really have an artist like you.' And I said – and this is so out of character for me, I would never usually say something like this – but I said, 'Nobody does.' That was rather confident of me."

Kylie celebrated the news with a huge 31st birthday bash in London attended by stars including Robbie Williams, Emma Bunton, Björk and Prince Naseem Hamed. The following month an art exhibition entitled simply 'Kylie Minogue by Rankin' ran for a month in The Strand, proving beyond doubt that Kylie had ascended the ranks of cultural icon of our times.

While Kylie considered what to present to Parlophone, she engaged in some acting work, determined to prove that her two Hollywood flops in no way represented her considerable talent. In mid-1999 she found herself in a most unlikely project, playing Miranda in a hip-hop production of *The Tempest* in Barbados.

"It's probably the most bizarre thing I've ever done, but it's very challenging," she said. "This role was a total surprise. A request came through asking if I'd like to be involved and it seemed so peculiar, not only to be doing Shakespeare, but to be doing it in Barbados as well! I couldn't say no. I met with the director and I was so terrified, I just said 'Look, let's get this straight, I've never done Shakespeare before. In fact, I've never done theatre before! Are you sure you've got the right girl?' He assured me it would be a lot of fun and a great experience, so here I am!"

After the event she was to admit, "Doing *The Tempest* in Barbados gave me the confidence boost I needed to open myself up to different opportunities. I'm busy doing all of this work but it's all building up to something bigger, like a feature film, and my next album, which I'm thinking about at the moment." *The Tempest* also led to a pleasant romantic sideline as Kylie went on to date her co-star Rupert Penry-Jones, an actor from the Royal Shakespeare Company also known as "the theatre-going woman's crumpet!"

"I don't want to say too much," teased Kylie at the time. "It's hard when you're seeing someone and it's early days, because you need to be left alone to get on with it. Let's just say I'm enjoying a romance – a romance as opposed to a relationship. I think as soon as you label something a relationship it puts pressure on and I don't want to do that. I'm having too much fun at the moment.

"I feel the happiest I've ever been."

"I bounce into work, my brother has come to live with me for a while and my sister's nearby, so we're always having family dinners. And I'm enjoying my romance right now. I feel it's finally my time. My lucky star's shining." Sadly the affair fizzled out due to Rupert's busy schedule – "it just wasn't to be" – but nothing could dampen Kylie's spirits.

Much of her happiness indeed stemmed from her family. Her brother Brendan, a TV cameraman, had moved into her Chelsea flat to keep her company and Dannii had recently taken on the lead role in the West End musical *Notre Dame De Paris*, so she too was nearby.

Nowadays Dannii was involved with Formula 1 racing driver Jacques Villeneuve and Kylie relished the chance to teach Dannii French, which she had picked up from Stephane Sednaoui, and spend time in her Paris apartment. "I've been teaching her the basic slushy words so she can be sweet with him," laughed the older sister. "She's picking it up. I like Jacques a lot. He's really sweet and they get on so well. They're very happy together." Soon Dannii and Jacques got engaged, and Kylie was delighted. "They are very well suited and they're madly in love. It was one of those things – boom! I wasn't jealous, more like wanting the same and thinking mmm ... that would be nice! I think it's wonderful."

That particular relationship would not go the distance, but this special time in Kylie's life afforded the sisters an opportunity to become very close. "We communicate better than we used to," she said of Dannii. "And we cry on each other's shoulder." Family was, as always, the most important aspect to her life, and Kylie endeavoured to visit her parents back in Australia twice a year, "for my Australian fix, which I need more as I get older. My poor parents have three kids living about as far away from them as you can possibly get, and they're very cool. I say there must be something wrong with them because they've never given any of us grief or pressure at all!"

Below: Congratulating her sister Dannii after her performance in *Notre Dame De Paris*

"I was sat in my kitchen with a friend, having just finished the best tour I'd ever done, and I was in need of a project to get me through the lull."

IN OCTOBER 1999 KYLIE BRAVED HER CRITICS BY publishing an expensive coffee-table book about herself. When questioned on her apparent self-indulgence, Kylie made no bones about her share of the proceeds going to charities in the UK and Australia.

Kylie: Evidence had been compiled over the last year with William Baker, and contained a series of Kylie's varied images dating from her appearances in *The Sullivans* to the present day. "It was borne out of a moment of boredom," she says. "I was sat in my kitchen with a friend, having just finished the best tour I'd ever done, and I was in need of a project to get me through the lull."

The tome contains both public and private shots of Kylie looking her best and also her worst. It opens with the disconcerting image of her old Madame Tussaud's waxwork; chipped, faded and disturbingly glassy-eyed. In amongst the other posed, candid and downright embarrassing shots were two particular images which made headlines. The first was a photo of her topless, taken in her dressing room after a performance at a gay club. "The reason I included that shot was because I remember the moment it was taken and I was so happy," she says. "But it's not there to shock, it's tasteful. It's a nipple. Big deal."

The other picture which caused so much fuss was a photograph of a fake tattoo on her arm reading: "I love Jason, Michael, Stephane" with a line scored through each name. "The list was a lot longer originally, but I had to narrow it down!" laughed the singer. "No, seriously, they were the three main loves of my life and they went hand in hand with the three biggest stages in my life, when I did the most changing as a person."

Evidence also included written contributions from artists and celebrities including Pet Shop Boys, Julie Burchill, Barry Humphries, Nick Cave, Shirley Manson, Nigel Kennedy, Vivienne Westwood, Bono and Jason Donovan. Kylie's personal favourite entry came from fellow Aussie, Clive James, who crowned her the "national thimble."

Aside from the charitable link, Kylie's reasoning behind the book was fairly clear cut. Having spent the past 20 years in the public eye, it was an attempt at self-analysis. "In general I don't like being forced to analyse things, I prefer not knowing, keeping some of the mystery. And once the book started becoming this analytical thing, it got more difficult," she admitted.

"I've found the whole thing really moving."

"For instance, there's a picture of Michael Hutchence and me with a young cancer patient who died shortly after that. Some of it is extremely emotional." On the whole though, the mood was kept upbeat. "For a long time, changing my image was almost the only way I had to express myself; I didn't have much of a say in my music. And I was good at it. I'm still good at it. What did I learn from this book? I'm still not sure!"

While doing the promotional rounds with *Evidence*, Kylie made headlines as she gamely French kissed rival pop star Geri Halliwell on Channel 4's *TFI Friday*. Geri was plugging her autobiography and the magic TV moment was captured after an impromptu arm wrestle between the girls to see whose book was best. Instant media reaction: shock, horror – was Kylie a lesbian?! "I've fancied other women," she tantalised, "but I haven't done anything about it."

Above and left: Kylie at the book launch for *Kylie: Evidence*, held at Selfridges, London

Above and far right: Dressed as Marilyn Monroe in *Gentlemen Prefer Blondes*, Kylie performs in Sydney Below: With Chris Evans on *TFI Friday*

Still, the newly created CampKylie relished playing with sexual stereotypes. After transforming herself into Marilyn Monroe to sing 'Diamonds Are A Girl's Best Friend' at the opening of Fox Studios in Sydney, Kylie enthused about Monroe's movie centred around a pair of unlikely transvestites.

First there was her cameo appearance as the Green Absinthe Fairy in *Moulin Rouge!* starring Nicole Kidman and Ewan McGregor, which would become a big hit upon its release the following year. "I was delighted when they asked me to get involved. I knew immediately it was something I'd

"My favourite film has to be Some Like It Hot. "

"It features what is probably Marilyn Monroe's finest screen performance, while Tony Curtis and Jack Lemmon – dressed as women – are simply hilarious."

A similar reference came with rumours that Kylie would play the daughter of Pet Shop Boy Neil Tennant in a gay musical set to debut at London's West End the following Christmas. Sadly this never came to pass, although Kylie's dulcet tones were heard on the duet 'In Denial' from the Pet Shop Boys' album, *Nightlife*.

Duets seemed the way forward as over the next year or so Kylie recorded 'The G House Project' with the Australian band Gerling for the album *When Young Terrorists Chase The Sun*, 'The Reflex' with cult Australian songwriter Ben Lee for an Australian-only Duran Duran tribute, and 'Bury Me Deep In Love' with The Triffids. There were also whispers concerning the singer working with Robbie Williams, ex-Take That star and current Prince of Pop.

If anyone were ever in doubt as to the identity of the Hardest Working Woman In Pop, Kylie proved her title admirably in 2000. While the contents of her forthcoming debut album for Parlophone remained a closely guarded secret, she chose to act in no less than three different Australian movies in her spare time.

love! My role is tiny, but it has given me the confidence to try acting again," said Kylie, who was also hired to record a song for the movie's soundtrack. "But when they edited the film, they cut out the bit where my song was meant to appear. So I'm no longer on the soundtrack, but I'm on screen."

Then along came *Sample People* and *Cut*. *Sample People* was a slick crime drama set in Sydney, and Kylie played Jess, the untrustworthy mistress of a wealthy drug lord. "*Sample People* was exactly what I had wished for," said Kylie. "It's an ensemble piece, Jess is an interesting character, it's set in Australia and it was driven by the filmmakers' enthusiasm and their belief in the project as opposed to having a lot of money." Kylie also performed a cover of Russell Morris' epic 'The Real Thing' on the soundtrack for the film, which premiered in May 2000.

If *Sample People* was the Aussie equivalent of *Pulp Fiction*, then *Cut* was their unabashed version of *Scream*. And why shouldn't Kylie try her hand at horror? Her 10-minute appearance sees her in the role of Eighties student film director Hilary Jacobs, who is working on a slasher movie called *Hot Blooded*. Hilary meets a grisly end when she is attacked by her psychotic boyfriend, wielding some nasty-looking garden shears. He promptly cuts out her tongue and places it on a table, before leaving her to die. It was quite an experience for our Kyles.

"We're having fun. It's very sweet and I don't want to put any pressure on it."

"I was doing screams and muffled noises and looking at my tongue lying on a kitchen table – which was peculiar," she recalls. "The next day I went to my singing coach. We were doing warm-up exercises and my coach said, 'It's really strange. Your tongue isn't doing what it should normally do.' I thought that was odd, then realised that the day before I'd been watching my tongue being pulled out. My brain must have absorbed this and thought my tongue wasn't there any more and stopped me being able to use it properly."

Although Kylie's roles in these films were mostly cameos, she was pleased with the experience.

"I have a lot of insecurities about my performances"

"but I guess that's why I keep going – I always want to be better," she reflected. "All actors are insecure. I think it's an inherent part of the profession. I wouldn't say I'm confident when it comes to acting in movies, and I make it even more difficult because I'm very hard on myself. So many aspects of my music involve acting but making a character believable is quite different and I need to remind myself of that all the time."

❤   ❤   ❤   ❤   ❤

Contrary to popular belief, Kylie Minogue met English model James Gooding in January 2000. They did *not* meet at the BRIT awards in March, and when James, seven years Kylie's junior, was growing up, he did *not* have posters of Kylie on his bedroom walls.

"We met in Los Angeles," says Kylie. "I don't know what it was like for him but he was there with a friend and we were introduced and I was just like, 'Oh, helllloooo!' But we saw each other lots before we actually started dating..." Despite excitable press conjecture that the couple were well on the way to marriage and parenthood, Kylie determined to play it cool with her "delightful scruff from Essex." They maintained separate apartments and a grown-up attitude. "We're having fun. It's very sweet and I don't want to put any pressure on it."

**Far left: Kylie with her "delightful scruff from Essex", James Gooding
Below left: At the *Moulin Rouge!* premiere
Below centre: At the *Q* Awards, 2000
Below right: At the opening of the Tate Modern, London**

Chapter 11: Spinning Around

"When he told me it was number one I just walked back into the room where all my friends were and started crying."

Eleven

Far right: Spinning around
Below and right: Another version of Kylie's gold hotpants, this time with tassels, at G-A-Y in the Astoria Club, London

IN JUNE 2000 KYLIE BURST BACK ONTO THE music scene with the release of her first single for Parlophone, 'Spinning Around'. It was an unashamed piece of sparkling disco pop and her best comeback yet, simultaneously entering both UK and Australian charts at number one.

"I was so relieved," she admits. "When my manager called me I couldn't take it in. I was playing backgammon at the time and he was teasing me saying, 'Go on, have a guess!' When he told me it was number one I just walked back into the room where all my friends were and started crying." 'Spinning Around' made Kylie history in the UK as not only was it her fifth solo number one and the 17th time she'd been in the Top 10, but it caused the singer to be listed in the *Guinness Book Of World Records* as The First Australian Female Solo Artist To Debut At Number One In The UK.

The massive success of 'Spinning Around' was aided not a little by a raunchy dance video in which Kylie displays her small-but-perfectly-formed derrière in a tiny pair of gold lamé hot pants which left little to the imagination.

"My friend found them at a market for about 50p and they've been in the back of my cupboard for about five years."

"They finally had an outing,"

smiled the singer. "One of my producers said he really liked that video for 'Some Kind Of Bliss' and when I asked why, he said, 'Well, it was the little denim hot pants.' So I made a mental note. The concept for the 'Spinning Around' video is basically people having fun in a night-club and I just thought: 'Hot pants!'"

While providing excellent tabloid fodder, female fans will be glad to know the revealing shorts exerted a modicum of insecurity from the flesh-flashing diva. Kylie warned the video's director, Dawn Shadforth, that she might tire of exposing her bum to the 200 extras at some point during the two-day shoot, and indeed she did.

"I just knew, being in those hot pants, and with the focus on me all day for two days, there was bound to be a minute when I just didn't feel like being on camera any more." Kylie reached the point where she became conscious of what she was (or rather, wasn't) wearing and yelled for some clothes

K

Above and far right: Unfazed by technical problems, Kylie sparkled at Party In The Park

to cover her temporarily. "The moment passed and we carried on but, as you can see, I have complexes too." As well as helping her single remain in the public's fascination for several months, the garment provided a lucrative business venture: Kylie was approached by fashion giants TopShop to design her own line of hot pants.

Kylie's bottom soon attracted more attention in the form of lads' mag, *GQ*. The unsuspecting singer posed for a series of photographs in a tennis outfit and was surprised to see herself on the cover the following month with her skirt hitched up and her G-string airbrushed out, as per the infamous Athena poster. Some sources claimed she was upset and considering suing for damages, but the truth was she found the whole debacle rather amusing.

"I had to laugh. I was looking through and... 'They've taken my knickers off!' I said it out loud! I think it's funny, really. I thought it was quite brave of them not to show my face and just have a picture of my bottom on the cover," she says. A year later, Kylie won an award for Services To Mankind at *GQ*'s Men Of The Year Awards.

❤ ❤ ❤ ❤ ❤

An awkward appearance at that summer's Party In The Park concert (during which the stage monitors broke, causing much embarrassment) did not detract the public's attention away from the Comeback Of The Year. Kylie's next single, 'On A Night Like This', was released in September 2000 with another sexy video, this time set in Monte Carlo and starring screen baddie, Rutger Hauer. Kylie modelled Versace and a set of diamonds so expensive that the shoot was attended by two

bodyguards. "The woman who delivered it said it was worth millions and millions, but never mentioned any currency," marvelled the singer. The song's parent album, *Light Years*, was also released in September and showcased Kylie's return to her pop roots, with a fair dose of disco included.

Initially entering both UK and Australian charts at number two, the album outsold all expectations, rapidly becoming her most popular since 1989's *Enjoy Yourself*. It sold four times platinum in her home country alone. Kylie's critics were silenced by its fresh and funky approach to dance music. Her campness was still in evidence but it was perhaps eclipsed by her newfound sense of humour and some well-thought out pop pairings.

"The whole thing felt like a summer holiday," said Kylie, comparing the recording of *Light Years* to the problematic *Kylie Minogue* II. "When I first met the different writers and producers for this one I said, 'These are my keywords: poolside, beach, cocktails and disco.' And I think we did it.

> *"I told every person who even considered working on this album that our intention was to have a laugh."*

Even the slightest hint of tension could get someone ejected from the studio!

"I wanted to get back to what I do best and I learned that lesson mainly from doing that tour in Australia. I could actually see for myself what the audience responded to, what they wanted. It was about re-establishing and reminding myself of what I do, how I do it, and generally indulging in the shininess, pinkness and campness of that side of my personality and of pop. And I loved it."

"Robbie said, all you need is some good songs. You've got everything else"

Below and far right: Performing 'Kids' with Robbie Williams at his show in Manchester

Undoubtedly part of *Light Years'* appeal was down to the primetime pairing of Kylie with Robbie Williams. Shortly after Kylie signed to Parlophone, Robbie (who shares her parent label, EMI) approached her with the idea of writing and recording some collaborations. "Robbie said, all you need is some good songs. You've got everything else," Kylie recalls. "He's very matter-of-fact like that."

The pair spent a few days in the countryside recording with Robbie's writing partner, Guy Chambers. The results were breathtaking. "Not only is Robbie a great pop star but he is a great songwriter," said Kylie. "He came up with the title 'Your Disco Needs You' and that's how that one happened. Then I said I'd love to have a song called 'Loveboat' and we did it. That simple." Alongside these tracks, Kylie also collaborated on 'I'm So High' with Chambers. And then there was 'Kids'...

The most anticipated duet in pop appeared on both Robbie's album *Sing When You're Winning* and *Light Years*, and was released as a single in October 2000. A flirtatiously suggestive video and some choice comments from the two singers soon provoked predictable rumours of romance.

"Kylie's smart, sweet and sexy," said Robbie. "I fancy her but I'm frightened of her. When we were in the studio together I was too scared to talk to her." Kylie denied all allegations with a smile, but enjoyed herself in the process. "I've always felt he was gorgeous, attractive and totally interesting," she said. "But we've been friends for so long, we can't really go back.

"My favourite moment with Robbie was when I appeared at his show in Manchester. It was priceless because Rob's so in control on stage, he's almost impossible to rattle. But he hadn't seen the dress I was going to wear – it was a little silver slip of a thing – but his face was absolutely beautiful because for a second he completely lost it. All the super-confidence was suddenly stripped away and he was like, 'Unnghh!' It was excellent. "

"*As soon as I was out of sight he was back in control but just for a minute there he was sweating.*"

The most anticipated duet in pop

Kylie's absolute favourite moment of 2000 was when she performed at the closing ceremony for the Olympics in Sydney on October 1. It was her biggest live audience to date and a jubilant occasion for both Kylie and her country. Dressed as a showgirl in huge pink feathers and sequins, she was spectacularly carried on stage on a surfboard held aloft by several strapping Australian football players.

in Europe to satisfy the overwhelming demand. Shortly thereafter, Kylie's management announced the tour would also extend to Australia and met with the same reaction, breaking all records when Kylie's eight shows at the Sydney Entertainment Centre sold out in under one hour, prompting a ninth concert to be added to her itinerary. Kylie would continue to make history with this leg of the tour,

> "*I was so desperate to be involved in the games because I was so proud that they were being held in my country*"

"Once I was on stage it was unbelievable. It's actually very hard for me to convey in words what it was like. I felt like I was in the middle of some weird special effect where you're dragged out of the dimension you're in.

"There were drag queens everywhere, prawns on bicycles, Elle Macpherson walking out on this massive camera lens ... it was just perfect. The whole stadium was dazzling. For a girl who loves anything that sparkles it was magical." Kylie performed several numbers including Abba's 'Dancing Queen', and went on to open the Paralympics a fortnight later.

After the massive build-up to the Olympics gig, Kylie went on a well-earned break on the northwest point of Australia. She stayed at an "amazing million-acre cattle station. I was feeling so Australian by that time. And I caught my own fish! This might sound stupid but to me it was one of my most satisfying achievements of the year: it was actually a barramundi, 65 cm long. Put up quite a struggle, I can tell you. And I ate it! Don't get me wrong, I love every aspect of my work and the attention but, man, catching that big, incredible fish was just the greatest."

Meanwhile, on the other side of the world, Kylie's fans were appeased with the release of *Hits+*, a collection of deConstruction singles, B-sides and previously unreleased recordings from that label. At around the same time she launched her official website, www.kylie.com, which she had been considering for years. Based on 'Spinning Around' and her favourite Manga comics, it featured a Kylie screensaver which was downloaded more than 70,000 times.

In November tickets were put on sale for Kylie's forthcoming On A Night Like This Tour, which would kick off in Glasgow in March 2001. It was to be her first full-scale tour of the UK for nearly a decade, and within hours all the dates had completely sold out. Extra appearances were then added, including some

playing to a quarter-of-a-million people in Australia alone; previously uncharted territory for a solo female performer.

Clearly on a roll, in December 2000 Kylie released the fourth single from *Light Years*, 'Please Stay', which reached number 10 in the UK. The position belied her fans' immediate reaction however, as they had hoped the flagrantly over-the-top 'Your Disco Needs You' would be next. In fact this track had been pencilled in as the first release for 2000 when it was recorded with Robbie Williams many months before. Although it became an instant favourite for Kylie's many gay followers when they heard it on *Light Years*, the outrageous song might have proved too much for her more conservative fans, so she instead opted for the safer 'Spinning Around'.

Nonetheless, 'Your Disco Needs You' soon became Kylie's unofficial anthem and she admitted it was one of her favourites too. "Camp doesn't begin to describe that song!" she laughs. "Camp in capital letters and neon lights still wouldn't do it justice. That song has always had a life of its own – it's so unique and has affected a lot of people. My favourite bit is when I sing, 'kick your ass' and the

**Far left: Singing 'Dancing Queen' at the Sydney Olympics 2000
Below: Joined on stage by a host of Australian stars later in the show**

Far left: Madonna honours Kylie at the MTV Awards
Left: Kylie at the TMF Awards

backing vocalists go, 'assss!' They had 10 male vocalists and they tracked them about three times so you've got 30 beefy vocalists going 'assss!' I think they were slightly embarrassed..."

Kylie finally relented to the unprecedented demand from fans' internet petitions and the like, releasing 'Your Disco Needs You' as a single in Germany and Australia in 2001. She even filmed an equally camp video starring a multitude of dancing bewigged Kylies to silence the protesters.

On November 16, 2000 Kylie received surely the ultimate style accolade – Madonna wore a T-Shirt emblazoned with sequins spelling out 'Kylie Minogue' during her performance at the European MTV Music Awards. When questioned on her choice of wardrobe, the veteran artiste said it was meant as a display of support for the Australian singer.

"That was surreal," said Kylie. She'd been present at the ceremony, performing 'Kids' with Robbie Williams and dressed in the daringly-cut silver Julien Macdonald dress that could reduce him to a whimper. "I was quite taken aback because I'd been like any other 15-year-old – wearing the lace gloves, following her career. I didn't think she'd even

heard of me. I met her briefly afterwards and she said, 'Did you like my T-shirt?' I said, 'Yes, very much!'

"*It was like being blessed by the Pope!*"

Kylie made a point of returning the compliment and wore a Madonna T-shirt in her next photo shoot.

Kylie celebrated Christmas in high style. Not a huge drinker, she had previously admitted to a penchant for tequila: "Time just disappears with tequila – it goes elastic and then vanishes". Her weakness was in evidence at a raucous festive party in London.

"The last time I remember being really inebriated was at a friend's party at Christmas," she confessed. "All these people were dancing in a room and I ended up crowd-surfing. I was hoisted up and passed around the room, while everyone was swaying below..." This appeared to be something of a special occasion for the former party animal, who continued, "But I don't party so much these days, and literally have to be tricked out of the house by my friends. All I want to do is pay the sleep bank."

115

Chapter 12: Can't Get You Out Of My Head

"When you get so much hype around you, your career can become very irritating. That's why you hear so many tales of drug addiction, alcoholism and the mad lifestyles of pop stars. I've always been lucky. It's never been really bad for me."

Far right: Kylie on *Top Of The Pops*

IN MARCH 2001 KYLIE EMBARKED ON HER ON A Night Like This Tour. Conceived as an all-singing, all-dancing night of pure entertainment, Kylie cavorted with her burly crew and wore a succession of skimpy costumes showing off her enviable figure. Having added endless extra dates, Kylie experienced problems with both her voice and her stamina and so consulted a vocal coach early on. Advised to keep up her energy levels by snacking on small pieces of chicken over the course of each concert, Kylie nearly came a cropper as a consequence. "One night I was singing 'Confide In Me', which is no walk in the park, and I could feel the chicken... hanging."

Always a workaholic, in tandem with the tour Kylie concentrated on other business ventures including charity modelling for Oxfam (stemming from her cheap gold hot pants) and the unveiling of her own underwear range, Love Kylie, for Australian manufacturer Holeproof. The latter she found particularly challenging as it was so far removed from anything she had done before. "I guess it just started out as something that would be fun," she said.

"The business side of it has been really interesting."

In tribute to Kylie's first worldwide hit, The Lucky Knicker (with the word 'Lucky' printed on it) was launched and soon became their biggest seller. Later in November, Kylie would auction off her own personal Lucky Knickers for Children In Need.

Amidst all this excitement, Kylie turned 33. As always she celebrated rather than hid her advancing years and in typical Minogue fashion pledged to somehow improve on her current success. "I'd like to get a lot better at what I do, I'd like to experiment a

lot more in life than talking about myself for the best part of each week, I'd like to travel in a way that involves seeing more than just the inside of TV studios," she enthused.

Although she would seem to be at the top of her game, the tour, business sidelines and work on the follow-up to *Light Years* provoked a certain anxiety. Kylie's greatest fear had always been loneliness, and somehow this was now heightened.

"You go out on stage and in front of you there are 10,000 people with this overwhelming admiration for you. You've been styled and look fabulous. The spotlight is on you, the dancers are all around you and for two hours you're the greatest woman there is. And then you get back to your hotel and ask: 'Any messages?' 'No, ma'am, no messages.' 'Faxes?' 'No.' 'Any e-mails?' 'No.' It's such a kick, then suddenly it's all over. That creates good grounds for uncertainty and depression. In the end, I just burst into tears."

Over the summer it all became too much and Kylie fell ill with exhaustion. After visiting the doctor she was told to take a week off to rest, no quibbles. "It was a blessing in disguise because it made people realise that I wasn't a machine that could just keep going," she said. "I needed reminding of that too. I'm the worst culprit – I just work, work, work. From now on I want to get more balance in my life, have more time for my family, friends, for me."

September 2001 saw the release of a new Kylie song, which would outshine anything else she'd ever recorded. So much for Kylie's determination to reclaim some balance to her life.

Co-written by former pop star Cathy Dennis, 'Can't Get You Out Of My Head' could have become a victim of its own hype. Much was made of the fact that it was released on the same day as Posh Spice

As always she celebrated rather than hid her advancing years

Victoria Beckham's solo single, 'Not Such An Innocent Girl'. Both singers engaged in all-out promotional campaigns and stylish hi-tech videos (Kylie's featuring the popstress almost wearing a ludicrously low-cut white hooded trouser suit).

To a certain extent both girls played to the gallery when quizzed on their competition, Kylie for example saying, "I really feel for Victoria at the moment. But she's a tough cookie. I imagine she can handle herself." Behind the scenes it was far friendlier, with Kylie sending Victoria a note assuring her all the posturing wasn't real. In the end, 'Can't Get You Out Of My Head' stayed true to its title as far as the public was concerned and stormed into the UK charts at number one, selling a staggering 306,000 copies to Victoria's meagre 45,000.

And that was only the beginning. The harder-edged, electronically-flavoured track with its cool, catchy chorus of 'La la la, la-la la la la' reached number one in every single Western European country (except Finland, where it stalled at number two). Worldwide it sold over 2.5 million copies.

If 2001 could be typified by one song alone, this was it.

"Entering at number one was just incredible," marvelled Kylie. "I was doing a TV show one morning and my record company has a number you can call which gives the week's chart results. My TV promo lady handed me the phone and the voice was saying, 'Kylie's entered at number one with sales of 306,000 copies.' It was like a movie moment. I couldn't speak and I handed her the phone and said, 'You have to listen because that can't be right.' I was flabbergasted."

The secret of the song's success was down to its understated effortlessness. "I fell in love with it the first time I heard the demo – it just gets to you," said Kylie. "I was so excited. I said, 'When can we do it? I'll do it today!'

'Can't Get You Out Of My Head' *because* **"I** *wish I'd written it's very simple – to the point that it's great."*

118

Kylie's desire to write the perfect pop song was soon realised in part. Hot on the heels of the single came the album, *Fever*, and Kylie had co-written several of its 12 excellent tracks.

Following directly on from the dance theme of *Light Years*, *Fever* was, if at all possible, slicker and more polished. Its songs were slightly more grown-up and clubbier rather than disco-flavoured. It was instantly as successful as 'Can't Get You Out Of My Head' and delighted everyone who heard it. Kylie was determined to stress that her masterpiece hadn't taken shape overnight.

"My success, which appears so sudden to everyone, took me two years of constant hard work to bring about. The worst thing is that you hope to come up with a number one hit. You think that, if you manage that, things will get easier, but they don't." One thing that Kylie noticed, perhaps for the first time, was the age difference between not only her and her fans but also her and her immediate chart competition: teenage superstars like Britney Spears and Christina Aguilera.

"I did *Top Of The Pops* recently," said Kylie, "and I looked around at the audience and thought, 'My God, I was doing this show before some of you were even born.'" She continued to say that Britney and Christina reminded her of when she started out. "The first thing that strikes me is how incredibly hard they must be working. They also seem a lot more mature and aware than I ever was. Maybe it's a generational thing – an 18-year-old today is a lot more savvy than I was at that age. I do find it quite astonishing that I'm still here, doing it. And I've done so much since I was 18, which is how old those girls are now. It's a whole lifetime."

“I haven't even had time to enjoy my success. I don't want to go out and drink champagne every night – I need some time out.”

"We do normal things like going to the cinema, going to the pub for a drink, going out for dinner or just lying on the couch watching TV. It's a nice, simple romance, which is great"

Dangerously for a while it seemed like Kylie's loneliness and exhaustion might make a reappearance. "I've climbed the ladder of success. Now I'm there, right at the top. But when I look around me from those dizzy heights, there's no one there except me. 'Hello? Where are my friends? Is my family still there? Why haven't I renovated my house yet?'"

With all the attention focused on Kylie, it was unsurprising that the media should start rumours about the state of her relationship with James Gooding, especially since he had recently been photographed holding hands with model Sophie Dahl, then kissing a "mystery brunette". For her part, Kylie was supposedly spotted in tears outside a restaurant.

"It was weird," said Kylie of this unhappy period.

"I have had to learn to deal with knowing what is real and what isn't."

Above: On stage at One Big Sunday
Far right: James Gooding does Kylie the world of good

"People say I'm unlucky in love, but it seems worse than it is. Even when it's wonderful, there's always something around the corner to test the partnership. Things with James are good but there aren't any rings on these fingers and we don't live together."

Even so, the next gossip to emerge was about the couple window-shopping for engagement rings in Spain, where Kylie was promoting *Fever*. Said Kylie, "I love James very much, but we're not getting married. Those stories are rubbish. I'm usually private about my relationships, but I just wanted to end those rumours."

In truth, James Gooding seemed to be living up to his name and was doing Kylie the world of good, and the singer wasn't afraid to address the constant stream of questions about their private life. "The fact he's younger than me doesn't mean he's not teaching me anything," she explained. "He's got quite a life behind him already. He's a wonderful person, I really love being with him and I can't wait to see him at the end of the day. We do normal things like going to the cinema, going to the pub for a drink, going out for dinner or just lying on the couch watching TV. It's a nice, simple romance, which is great. And I want to keep it that way."

James, who had previously danced in the music video for Madonna's 'Bedtime Story', benefited from the attention and his modelling career took off. He was seen in no less than three UK TV adverts running concurrently; for Wella hair products, Archers drinks and the Hugo Deep Red fragrance. Still, Kylie often made it clear that her current boyfriend hailed from a different world to many of her exes, and wasn't in the least bit showbiz.

"James isn't really interested in that world. He'll come to a show, he'll be proud and pleased and hopefully enjoy it, but he just doesn't need to know too much about it. It's very refreshing for me. He's so down-to-earth and he's not easily impressed. When my life gets a bit hectic, he's very patient and that's great."

Perhaps in her thirties Kylie was beginning to get on a bit for a pop star, and at this time no interviewer left a meeting with her without posing some very repetitive questions about her plans for marriage and children. Regarding the former, Kylie revealed, "I've never been properly proposed to! But that doesn't make me feel sad, because normally I'm walking away from something – it's fear of commitment. I have felt settled three times, but for whatever reason, they didn't carry on. I don't regard any of them as failures. No matter how long they go, you get something positive out of them."

Interestingly those "three" relationships always referred to Jason, Michael and Stephane, seemingly without regard for James' feelings. However, when it came to finding a father for her children, the media wondered if they were onto a winner.

"People come up to me and say, 'Come on Kyles, when's it going to happen, when are you going to get pregnant?' I hate to disappoint them, but not any time soon! I'd *like* to have children and I used to say I'd *definitely* have children but I'm not so sure now. What's meant to be, will be. I think it's already written.

two albums and all the sidelines, his daughter had made the most stunning showbiz comeback in history. Although she donated her £150,000 Agent Provocateur fee to charity, when the *Sunday Times* published its annual list of the UK's highest earners this year, it was revealed Kylie had made £4.25 million *after* tax.

No one could dispute that 2001 had been Kylie's best year yet, and it was topped off nicely in December when she was honoured twice at the Top Of The Pops awards. Beating off stiff competition from Madonna and Atomic Kitten among others, Kylie scooped Top Tour and Top Single.

"Y*ou work and work and work and then go, 'Oh, I'm 33. If I'm going to have children, I need to think about that.'*"

"Everything's going well, but where do I really want to go? Am I just going to keep climbing the ladder of success? What's up there?"

For the next few months there was no escaping Ms Minogue, who appeared to have taken over certain TV channels as well as radio airwaves. In October she appeared in an ITV special, *An Audience With Kylie Minogue*, in which she notably duetted with Kermit the Frog (yes, really) on 'Especially For You'. Then she copied her boyfriend and filmed an advert for Eurostar; travelling to Paris and teasing fans by trying on a voluminous white wedding dress. Kylie could also be heard three times a week singing 'Always Forever', the theme tune to the new ITV soap, *Night And Day*.

Kylie then switched her attention to the cinema and appeared in a raunchy trailer advertising Agent Provocateur underwear. The commercial, which was deemed too racy for TV, saw every man's dream woman initially clad in the pink nurse's uniform worn by Agent Provocateur's shop assistants and designed by Vivienne Westwood. She strips off for the camera and lives out various fantasies including riding a red velvet bucking bronco. As a sex kitten, Kylie had surpassed herself. "I actually stopped breathing when I saw the first edit," she said. "I thought, I hope my dad's not going to see it. It's such a fine line between looking cheap and too full-on... I thought, I've really outdone myself this time. It's like I don't know what I'm doing."

Whatever Ron Minogue had to say about the situation, there was no denying that with the last

One month later she was nominated for no less than four BRIT awards for Best Pop Act, Best Video ('Kids' with Robbie), Best International Album and Best International Female. Kylie would indeed win two of the four awards; Best International Female and Best International Album, and performed at the ceremony. It was incredible. Even the planned second release from Fever, 'In Your Eyes', had to be postponed due to continuing demand for 'Can't Get You Out Of My Head.'

Kylie's status was now so great that she had Michael Jackson writing for her. He apparently offered two tracks, 'I'll Try Anything Once' and 'Time Bomb' for inclusion on a US-only album which would comprise the best tracks from *Fever* and *Light Years*. 'Can't Get You Out Of My Head' had prevented Jackson's own comeback single, 'You Rock My World', from hitting the top UK chart position and America was suddenly interested in Kylie for the first time since 'The Loco-Motion' was at number three in 1988.

But Kylie remained cool and non-committal. After all – she had travelled this far, why on earth should she start from scratch?

"The US is knocking on my door and I'm not answering it yet," she said. "They're all very excited about 'Can't Get You Out Of My Head'. I've had the biggest cheese and the second biggest cheese and then another big cheese from EMI all asking about America... a cheese platter! I guess because I've been there before and experienced that, the thought of having to explain how you say my name and tell my soap opera beginnings again and again to Midwestern stations is more than I can bear..."

Far left and below: Kylie won two awards at the BRITs in 2002

The main thing about Kylie Minogue is that she's 'nice'

Outro

> "**I** *don't like plans. Someone once said if you want to make God laugh, tell him your plans – and I believe that. I'm a fatalist.*"

IN OCTOBER 2001 PARLOPHONE RELEASED A press statement boasting that Kylie's 2002 UK tour had outsold Madonna's UK dates for her own Drowned World Tour earlier that year. Kylie's concerts took in more of Britain than ever before and kept her busy from the last week of April to the end of May.

Truly an icon of her time, Kylie's life has recently inspired a stage show, called *I Should Be So Lucky*. In the style of *Mamma Mia!*, the West End hit based on the music of Abba, the romantic comedy uses 25 of Kylie's songs to create a story about a gay man (rather cheesily named Scott and played by Damien Aylward) searching for Mr Right. The show ran in Melbourne in spring 2002, with further plans to bring it to London.

looks forward to being 40, stating, "I'll be a woman by then. I want to age gracefully – the disgraceful part will be in private!"

Would she ever consider retiring? "I have thought about it, but I'm not sure what I'd do instead," she admits. "I think I'd miss singing too much. But will I still be going strong in 10 years? I don't know. I don't like plans. Someone once said if you want to make God laugh, tell him your plans – and I believe that. I'm a fatalist."

The secret to her success, as far as Kylie's concerned, is simple. "I'm not brilliant at one thing," she says. "It's a mixture – I look alright, I can sing alright. I can dance reasonably well. "

Far left and below: Kylie has no plans for retirement

> "**P**eople can relate to me *because I'm not out of reach or unattainable. It's a kind of ordinariness.*"

What more could Kylie possibly have in store for her fans after the overwhelming success of the last two years? She has said that she would like to do some more acting, perhaps try her hand at film producing, or even follow her sister Dannii onto the stage with a musical of her own. Equally, many have surmised that she's due for some well-earned time off – a viewpoint with which Kylie readily agrees: "I just want to look after myself for a while. I'd like to live without the pressure that has always surrounded me. I need to find out who I am. You know, not see a mirror for a year. Not present myself, not even care about appearance or perception because that's been on my shoulders for so many years.

"But don't think I'm having a huge crisis," she assures us. "That's not the case." Unbelievable as it may seem for those who grew up with her, Kylie now

Showgirl aside, the main thing about Kylie Minogue is that she's 'nice'. A bland word in itself, it sums her up perfectly, stripping her bare of any garish costume or provocative posing and is the exact reason she has lasted in the public eye as long as she has. In 1998, when *Q* magazine famously asked her to pick five words to describe herself, she gave us,

> "**I**nquisitive. **T**hankful. **F**lippant. **L**oving. **H**appy "

and that's probably the most accurate description of her sunny personality there is.

Discography

Albums

Kylie!
1988

I Should Be So Lucky
The Loco-Motion
Je Ne Sais Pas Pourquoi
Got To Be Certain
Turn It Into Love
I Miss You
I'll Still Be Loving You
Look My Way
Love At First Sight

Enjoy Yourself
1989

Hand On Your Heart
Wouldn't Change A Thing
Never Too Late
Nothing To Lose
Tell-Tale Signs
My Secret Heart
I'm Over Dreaming (Over You)
Tears On My Pillow
Heaven And Earth
Enjoy Yourself

Rhythm Of Love
1990

Better The Devil You Know
Step Back In Time
What Do I Have To Do?
Secrets
Always Find The Time
The World Still Turns
Shocked
One Boy Girl
Things Can Only Get Better
Count The Days
Rhythm Of Love

Let's Get To It
1991

Word Is Out
Just Give Me A Little More Time
Too Much Of A Good Thing
Finer Feelings
If You Were With Me Now
Let's Get To It
Right Here, Right Now
Live And Learn
No World Without You
I Guess I Like It Like That

Kylie Minogue
1994

Confide In Me
Surrender
If I Was Your Lover
Where Is The Feeling
Put Yourself In My Place
Dangerous Game
Automatic Love
Where Has The Love Gone?
Falling
Time Will Pass You By

Impossible Princess
(Retitled Kylie Minogue)
1997

Too Far
Cowboy Style
Some Kind Of Bliss
Did It Again
Breathe
Say Hey
Drunk
I Don't Need Anyone
Jump
Limbo
Through The Years
Dreams

Intimate And Live
1999

Too Far
What Do I Have To Do?
Some Kind Of Bliss
Put Yourself In My Place
Breathe
Take Me With You
I Should Be So Lucky
Dancing Queen
Dangerous Game
Cowboy Style
Step Back In Time
Say Hey
Free
Drunk
Did It Again
Limbo
Shocked
Confide In Me
The Loco-Motion
Should I Stay Or Should I Go
Better The Devil You Know

Hits+
2000

Confide In Me
Put Yourself In My Place
Where Is The Feeling?
Some Kind Of Bliss
Did It Again
Breathe
Where The Wild Roses Grow
If You Don't Love Me
Tears
Gotta Move On
Difficult By Design
Stay This Way
This Girl
Automatic Love
Where Has The Love Gone?
Take Me With You

Light Years
2000

Spinning Around
On A Night Like This
So Now Goodbye
Disco Down
Loveboat
Koocachoo
Your Disco Needs You
Please Stay
Bittersweet Goodbye
Butterfly
Under The Influence Of Love
I'm So High
Kids
Light Years

Fever
2001

More More More
Love At First Sight
Can't Get You Out Of My Head
Fever
Give It To Me
Fragile
Come Into My World
In Your Eyes
Dancefloor
Love Affair
Your Love
Burning Up

Discography

Singles

The Loco-Motion – 1987
I Should Be So Lucky – 1988
Got To Be Certain – 1988
The Loco-Motion – 1988
Je Ne Sais Pas Pourquoi – 1988
Especially For You (with Jason Donovan) – 1988
Turn It Into Love – 1988
It's No Secret – 1989
Hand On Your Heart – 1989
Wouldn't Change A Thing – 1989
Never Too Late – 1989
Tears On My Pillow – 1990
Better The Devil You Know – 1990
Step Back In Time – 1990
What Do I Have To Do? – 1991
Shocked – 1991
Word Is Out – 1991
If You Were With Me Now (with Keith Washington) – 1991
Keep On Pumpin' It (Visionmasters with Tony King
featuring Kylie Minogue) – 1991
Give Me Just A Little More Time – 1992
Finer Feelings – 1992
What Kind Of Fool (Heard It All Before) – 1992
Celebration – 1992
Confide In Me – 1994
Put Yourself In My Place – 1995
Where Is The Feeling – 1995
Where The Wild Roses Grow (with Nick Cave) – 1995
Some Kind Of Bliss – 1997
Did It Again – 1998
Breathe – 1998
German Bold Italic (with Towa Tei) – 1998
Cowboy Style – 1998
Spinning Around – 2000
On A Night Like This – 2000
Kids (with Robbie Williams) – 2000
Please Stay – 2000
Your Disco Needs You – 2001
Can't Get You Out Of My Head – 2001
In Your Eyes – 2002

Compilations

12-Inch Remix Collection – 1991
Best Remixes Volume 2 – 1992
Kylie's Remixes Volume 1 – 1993
Kylie's Remixes Volume 2 – 1993
Non-Stop History – 1993
Remix Volume 1 – 1993
Remix Volume 2 – 1993
Greatest Hits – 1994
Greatest Hits – 1998
Impossible Remixes – 1998
50+1 – 1998
Greatest Remix Hits Volume 1 – 1998

Videos

The Videos – 1988
The Kylie Collection – 1988
The Videos 2 – 1989
On The Go – 1991
Let's Get To It ...The Videos – 1992
Kylie Live! – 1992
Live In Dublin – 1992
Greatest Hits – 1992
Greatest Video Hits – 1993
The Kylie Tapes – 94-98 – 1998
Greatest Hits – 1998
Intimate & Live – 1999
Live In Sydney – 2000